Counselling by Telephone

PROFESSIONAL SKILLS FOR COUNSELLORS

The *Professional Skills for Counsellors* series, edited by Colin Feltham, covers the practical, technical and professional skills and knowledge which trainee and practising counsellors need to improve their competence in key areas of therapeutic practice.

Titles in the series include:

Medical and Psychiatric Issues for Counsellors
Brian Daines, Linda Gask and Tim Usherwood

Personal and Professional Development for Counsellors
Paul Wilkins

Counselling by Telephone
Maxine Rosenfield

Time-Limited Counselling
Colin Feltham

Client Assessment
Stephen Palmer and Gladeana McMahon (eds)

Counselling, Psychotherapy and the Law
Peter Jenkins

Counselling by Telephone

Maxine Rosenfield

SAGE Publications
London • Thousand Oaks • New Delhi

SAGE Publications Ltd
6 Bonhill Street
London EC2A 4PU

SAGE Publications Inc.
2455 Teller Road
Thousand Oaks, California 91320

SAGE Publications India Pvt Ltd
32, M-Block Market
Greater Kailash – I
New Delhi 110 048

British Library Cataloguing in Publication data

A catalogue record for this book is available
from the British Library.

ISBN 0 8039 7998 3
ISBN 0 8039 7999 1 (pbk)

Library of Congress catalog card number 96-070928

Typeset by Mayhew Typesetting, Rhayader, Powys
Printed in Great Britain by Hartnolls Ltd, Bodmin, Cornwall

Contents

Foreword

'. . . it gave me self-confidence to know someone was listening to me.'
A child ringing ChildLine

The Telephone Helplines Association came into existence in March 1996. Its forerunner of almost 10 years, The Telephone Helplines Group, had pioneered standards in telephone counselling including the publication of *Guidelines for Telephone Helplines* and *Evaluation of Telephone Helplines*. This group based its work on the experience of a large number of very diverse telephone helplines, covering an enormous range of help, advice and information for adults, the elderly and children and young people who come from every possible background and perspective. The publication of *Counselling by Telephone* is, therefore, timely, bringing together a vast amount of information and experience about telephone helplines, which has been accumulated in the last decade. It is a source book for those wishing to find information about how counselling by telephone works in different settings – the many case examples provided are particularly useful. It also helps the reader to think about the complex practical, theoretical (counselling/therapy) and ethical issues involved in setting up and providing services by telephone.

Maxine Rosenfield's book represents the most comprehensive statement about telephone counselling in the UK to date and, as such, is to be welcomed as a significant milestone in the development of telephone counselling as an activity in its own right. A caller to a telephone helpline summarised how important a telephone service is to her: *'I can pick up the phone whenever I need to and so what matters most to me is that someone has the time, someone has the will, to listen when I need to be heard.*' This book will help us all to structure our will to listen, to manage our helplines, to make the most helpful response to callers and to provide the best possible service for those who seek our help.

Hereward D.M. Harrison
Director of Children's Services
ChildLine UK
Member of Telephone Helplines Association Executive Committee
18 September 1996

Acknowledgements

Many people have generously, willingly and openly talked with me and shared their resources and experiences to enable this book to be written.

In particular, I am grateful to the hours spent in discussion and meetings with Luci Allen of NSPCC, Simon Armson of The Samaritans, Nicola Barden, Fod Barnes of OFTEL, Norman Barnfather, Wolf Blomfield, Francine Bradshaw, Dr Elizabeth Bryan of Multiple Births Foundation, Emma Fletcher, Hereward Harrison of ChildLine, Alan Jamieson of the British Association for Counselling, Annie Morgan, Liz Nichols, Sarah Pitman, Barbara Read of Multiple Births Foundation, Sandra Ridley of CareAssist, Adrian Scarfe of the Spinal Injuries Association, Liz Urben of Cancerlink, Terry Veitch of Community Network, Susan Wallbank of CRUSE, Claire Wheeler of The Princess Royal Trust Camden Carers Centre, Charlotte Willoughby and Chris Wynne-Davies of BT.

In thanking those whose contributions are quoted and referred to in the book, I also wish to thank those, too numerous to name, whose conversations and debates have further aided my work.

Introduction

Can counselling be done by phone? If you had posed that question to a group of people working on a variety of helplines in the late 1980s, most of them would have replied with a resounding 'No!' Just five years later, the question was discussed at seminars organised for Broadcasting Support Services and the answer each time was a resounding 'Yes!' What was it that happened, in that short period, to change so dramatically the views of a random sample of workers across the helpline world?

There are two, separate, key contributing factors. Firstly, the use of the telephone and rapid, recent advances in telecommunications technology have together made the telephone a more acceptable and a more accessible medium for communication in the UK among all age groups. With a telephone, geographical and physical barriers to some help and support can be reduced. In addition, technology has improved the quality of the sound connection, with fewer crackling lines and better microphones and earpieces in the phones themselves, which can often be adjusted to suit an individual's hearing level. The explosion in the use of mobile phones is surely evidence that more and more people want to communicate by telephone, wherever they might happen to be.

Secondly, the proliferation of training courses has made counselling qualifications more accessible, financial considerations permitting. Some counsellors working face to face also work for groups or organisations which provide a telephone helpline and so have been able to transfer and adapt their face to face skills to the medium of the telephone. Two results of this rise in popularity of counselling training and the proliferation of counsellors offering their services are that 'counsellor-speak', the jargon of counselling such as paraphrasing, empathy and reflection, has become more widely used and the concept of the counsellor is more familiar to the public at large. For example, after a major disaster it is now common to see or to hear reported on the news that 'counsellors have been brought in to work with the survivors . . .'.

Seeking out support and help has also become more acceptable across many groups and communities; this is easily demonstrated by looking through directories of helping agencies or at notice-boards in public libraries where one can see that there has been a rapid expansion of self-help and support groups for people suffering from a particular illness or experiencing a particular situation. Alongside this, asking for counselling has also become more acceptable and less stigmatised for many people. So, putting together the greater access to and use of the telephone with a wider acceptance of counselling, it is not hard to see why counselling by telephone is on the increase.

Communication by telephone in a supportive capacity can be divided into two distinct areas, *counselling* by telephone and using *counselling skills* on the phone. In reality, these two types of relationships complement each other. If a counsellor has the skills and ability to enter into a formal counselling relationship on the phone, then that same counsellor should also be able to take a step or two sideways from that formal relationship and transfer their expertise in order to conduct one-off relationships with different callers, such as would be experienced by many seeking help from helplines. This is because *counselling* in the sense of experiencing a formal practical and theoretical training and working to obtain a qualification prior to setting up a counselling practice encompasses *counselling skills*, which all those who are counsellors must surely have developed during their training in order to be practitioners. While researching and writing this book, I came to realise that counselling and counselling skills overlap greatly in telephone work and therefore to focus on one without the other would be incomplete. Most of the case studies reflect this overlap and illustrate the different emphases which can be given to counselling and counselling skills within the context of telephone work.

Many counsellors have adapted their face to face skills and theoretical knowledge in order to work effectively by phone, while helpline workers *must* be using counselling skills to some degree in their telephone work, whether or not the skills are formally taught and recognised as such. Indeed some helpline workers have gone on to train as counsellors. This cross-fertilisation of practices, awareness and skills further highlights and encourages the overlap.

The obvious advantages for some people in using the telephone for counselling will be referred to in the book. For example, housebound clients may be better served by telephone counselling than by someone visiting them at home. People in some rural communities may have no access to local counsellors; others may not wish to use local counsellors even if they are available. The telephone offers the potential for working with people who live anywhere, within or outside of the UK.

Some counsellors do not believe that the telephone can be an effective counselling medium: 'If you cannot see the person you miss out on so much' is often quoted to me. Yet psychoanalysis, for example, does not always employ face to face contact such as when the analysand is lying on a couch although the analyst will probably sense the person's presence. It might be that some counsellors feel defensive about counselling by telephone because it breaches natural counselling defences by challenging some of the boundary issues which face to face counselling uses. For example, as will be seen in this book, a telephone counselling client has what might be described as the ultimate power over the counsellor – the client can terminate the call at any time by hanging up, which is an easier action to take than physically walking out of the room. This reluctance to embrace the telephone has until recently been endorsed, perhaps inadvertently, by counselling and therapeutic authorities who have not acknowledged telephone work as a counselling medium. The British Association for Counselling (BAC) has now started to acknowledge telephone counselling through its National Vocational Qualification process from 1994 onwards and in 1996 through setting up a special working party to consider the inclusion of some work by telephone in the accreditation of counsellors who work face to face and by phone. This development has been driven by a few committed individuals and is to be applauded.

In all my recent work with numerous telephone helplines and with counselling services around the UK, I have found no evidence to suggest that those answering the phone think that their work is less valuable than face to face work. Indeed, many helplines take an integrative perspective with the caller and if they are discussing options for that caller to seek further help, it might encompass telephone or face to face support from that service or other agencies. Helplines have been in existence for several decades. The Samaritans, perhaps one of the best-known telephone services is now over 40 years old, which means it was operating long before the popularisation of counselling. The quantity and range of telephone helpline services has increased dramatically in recent years. The first ever UK *Directory of Helplines* was launched in 1996 by the Telephone Helplines Association. It lists some 800 national, regional and local services which claim to follow accepted *helpline standards* for good practice. If there were no need or useful role for such services, they would not continue to exist.

All helplines use *counselling skills* to some degree in their work. Very few offer *counselling*. This book aims to illustrate those aspects which make telephone counselling distinct from both face to face counselling and from telephone helpline work, as well as covering areas of similarity. It highlights the skills needed to supplement a counselling qualification to carry out effective telephone counselling and will consider the benefits to both client and counsellor of working by phone. It will also consider a relatively new concept: group counselling by phone. In addition, the book will discuss some of the technical and practical implications of telephone work. Counselling by letter, counselling by E-mail and counselling in other media are discussed briefly in the final chapter, since these types of counselling are already being carried out and no doubt will develop further in time.

Most counsellors will experience some telephone contact with clients such as the first contact, when a client is in a crisis or when a client cancels a session. Each of these conversations requires a counsellor to be aware of the attitude, behaviour and manner conveyed when talking with the client and its possible impact on the client. Counselling by telephone extends and develops these areas of awareness within an integrated theoretical framework.

During the two years that this book was being written there were significant changes in telecommunications technology in particular. These are being modified and developed and are leading to further changes. It is essential that the world of counselling open its eyes and ears and minds to new options which enable 'traditional' counselling to be adapted to take account of technology which might suit our clients far better than the 'traditional' choices. This book seeks to encourage all counsellors to think again.

1

What is Counselling by Telephone?

In simple terms, counselling by telephone may be defined as a service whereby a trained counsellor works with a client, or a group of clients, by telephone, to enable the client(s) to explore personal situations, problems or crises in a one-off or in an on-going longer term therapeutic relationship.

A contract of some sort is agreed between the counsellor and client(s) and there may be a financial relationship as well, particularly for ongoing work.

Since counsellor and client are unlikely ever to meet in almost all cases of counselling by telephone, some time must be taken, during a preliminary session perhaps, for both parties to get used to each other's voice tones, accents, patterns of speech and other aspects of contact which would be obvious or easily integrated if they met, such as visual impressions of each other or a sense of the physical surroundings where the sessions take place.

Not all counsellors will find that they are able to work effectively on the phone. Of course, this does not mean that they are any less effective as face to face counsellors; simply that the telephone medium does not suit them.

Similarly, not all clients have a telephone and nor will all potential clients find the telephone a comfortable medium. A report from OFTEL (1994) stated that those households least likely to have a telephone are those in lower socio-economic groups, those headed by an economically inactive person or those on a low income. On the other hand, according to the 1992 General Household Survey (OPCS, 1992), 89 per cent of the population of the UK in 1992 had a telephone in their home, compared with 72 per cent in 1980 and 42 per cent in 1972, so the telephone has clearly become an increasingly popular, readily accessible and familiar tool.

There are, of course, other, more common reasons than counselling for working with people on the phone:

- advice may be offered
- advocacy may be provided
- information may be provided
- support can be offered
- befriending can take place

The continuum of the relationship between the different methods of working by telephone:

Advice → ← Advocacy → ← Information → ← Counselling → ← Support → ← Befriending

---

For the purposes of this book, my definitions of these are as follows:

Advice giving

This is when the caller is offered a course of action to follow. In response to a question or a situation being explained by the caller, action can be suggested. It might be phrased as 'If I were you I'd . . .' or 'You must do . . .'

By way of example, a call to a gas company, when someone thinks there may be a gas leak, would lead to advice being given:

Gas Company: Gas Service Emergency Line. How may I help you?

Caller: I think I can smell gas in the kitchen and I don't have a gas cooker, or anything using gas except the heating.

Gas Company: How long is it since you noticed this?

Caller: Since I got up this morning. It's getting stronger.

Gas Company: You must turn off your supply until someone can come and check it. In the meantime, don't strike a match or switch on a light or do anything that could cause a spark. Do you know how to switch off your supply?

Caller: Yes.

> *Gas Company*: OK, can I have your details please so that I can arrange for someone to come round?
> *Caller*: Yes, it's . . .
> *Gas Company*: Someone will be there within two hours.
> *Caller*: Thank you. Goodbye.

So here is a straightforward call with the caller seeking advice from someone with more knowledge about the issue.

Advocacy

This requires the person answering the phone to support and to act on behalf of the caller, or perhaps on behalf of the person the caller is talking about in the case of a child protection helpline. To be an advocate, the person answering the call has to have knowledge of the issue being discussed and be able to interpret or assess needs as well as knowing how to progress the enquiry.

Taking the example of a child protection telephone service, at the NSPCC Child Protection Helpline the person answering the phone may advocate on behalf of the caller or on behalf of the child about whom the caller is speaking. If the caller is an adult and is talking about a child whom the helpline counsellor perceives to be at risk, the counsellor is able to refer information to local social services, for example, whether or not the caller agrees, although clearly every effort is made first to try to gain the caller's co-operation in such situations. The Helpline's primary responsibility is to advocate on behalf of a child.

> *Child Protection Helpline (CPH)*: Hello, this is the Child Protection Helpline.
> *Caller*: I don't know if I should be calling . . . you see I'm very concerned about a child in a particular situation. Can I speak to you in confidence?
> *CPH*: Yes you can speak in confidence, but if you give us details of a child who is at risk, we have a responsibility to act to ensure the protection of the child. Would you like to give me a general idea of what your concerns are?
> *Caller*: I'm a grandmother and the child lives with its mother. Its father is my son and we have concerns about how the child is being looked after . . . .
> *CPH*: Can you give me some detail of what are your actual concerns and perhaps tell me when you last saw the child . . . ?

The CPH counsellor needs to establish how urgent the concerns might be. Using counselling skills to work with the caller, the counsellor must explore the situation in order to be able to make a judgement, there and then, of how to focus the call, on the basis of the information received. So in the above example, the counsellor would possibly move on to establish whether the grandmother's concerns are significant enough to indicate that the child might be at risk. If the counsellor perceives that this is the case, the counsellor might then try to encourage the grandmother to willingly disclose more information in the child's interests so that action to protect the child can be taken.

Information

This is the delivery of facts about a situation, in answer to a question or presenting circumstances. Although requiring a friendly tone of voice, there is no engaging in any in-depth conversation except for further clarification of what has been said. The person answering the call must have, or be able to access readily, the information sought. A welfare benefits enquiry to a carer's service may offer this type of service.

Carers' worker: Hello, this is the carers centre.

Caller: Hello, I wonder if you can answer a question I have. . . .

Carers' worker: I'd be pleased to help if I can. . . .

Caller: I'm sure it's very simple, in fact I think I was told, but I can't remember. . . . The person I am caring for has been in hospital for five weeks. Does her attendance allowance stop?

Carers' worker: Yes, it stops after four weeks.

Caller: I see. That's what I thought. Does this happen automatically?

Carers' worker: No, you have to inform the attendance allowance unit and send the payment book to them.

Caller: Right. . . .

Carers' worker: Were you wanting to know about anything else?

Caller: Well, I saw a notice on the board at the library – that's how I got your number – and it said you run support groups for carers. Could you tell me a bit about that?

Carers' worker: Yes, of course. We run a group every Friday morning from 10 until 12 at the health centre and one on a Tuesday afternoon from 2 until 4 p.m. at the library meeting room. Both are drop-ins, so you can turn up whenever you find it convenient. We also run some special carers' meetings here at the centre on topics like Community Care and if you like I could add you to our mailing list for information. . . .

Caller: Yes, that would be good. Meeting other carers could help me to feel less isolated. My name is _____ and I live at _____

Carers' worker: OK, I'll send you information and look forward to seeing you at one of the drop-ins perhaps, or at a meeting here. . . .

Caller: Thank you. That's been really helpful. I will see you soon, I'm sure. Goodbye.

Carers' worker: Goodbye.

A straightforward request for information is made by the caller. The worker answers the question and because the caller seems to hesitate, checks out whether the caller might have been wanting anything else. This enables the caller to move on to talk further and to ask questions. The worker answers and leaves space for the caller to talk further in case the caller wants to, but in the above example, information was all that was wanted.

Many helplines will report that calls to the service often present themselves as an initial enquiry requesting information. If the worker provides openings in case there are any other issues to be discussed, as happened above, the caller can choose to take them up or not.

Support

This involves responding with empathy to a caller. Some people have this ability quite naturally but others do not and I would question whether it can be distinctly taught for application to the telephone, or indeed for face to face work. I do not believe counsellors can be *taught* the instinct of empathy; rather they are born with the natural instinct and training enables them to develop an awareness of the instinct and how to use it with a client. If the fundamental instinct to be able to be alongside someone without jumping in to offer sympathy, an opinion or instruction is lacking, a person is unlikely to be able to modify their attitude over the telephone. This is because the person does not have the visual clues which might otherwise warn them, if they could see the impact their remarks were having, that they were not responding appropriately.

Telephone support may be sought either from someone who has been through a similar experience to oneself, that being their primary 'qualification', or from someone who has detailed knowledge and awareness of a particular situation and an ability to empathise. Many helpline services advertise that they offer support, which I believe means using counselling skills to listen, empathise with the caller and perhaps provide factual information or details of other specialised agencies with whom the caller might wish to make contact for additional support or help. Whether offering support based on professional training or on personal experience, the supporter must be clearly aware of when their professional or personal experience of the situation can become a limiting factor in the support that they can offer. In other words, there must be awareness of the boundaries or limits of the service which can be offered and knowing when it could be more helpful for the caller to also talk to other people or to consider alternative suggestions.

Self-help groups may offer a supportive type of telephone service:

Caller: Is that the Eastbridge breast cancer support group?

Supporter: Yes, I'm Maria. How can I help?

Caller: Well, it says in your leaflet, that I got from the hospital, that you're there to support and help people who have cancer. I've just been told that I have got breast cancer . . . and I'm really scared. What will happen?

Maria: It is very hard to be told that you have cancer and there can be lots of things to think about. . . .

Caller: Have you had cancer?

Maria: Yes, I had breast cancer four years ago.

Caller: How did you feel? Were you scared? I can't believe it is happening to me . . . I'm so frightened. . . .

Maria: It is a very difficult time. What have you been told?

Caller: [*crying*] I'm so scared . . . all you think about is that that's it, the end . . . I'm sorry for crying. . . .

Maria: Mmmm, it's OK, take your time . . . it is quite natural to be worried . . . has anyone at the hospital suggested any treatment?

Caller: Yes, they say I've got to have the lump taken out and then four weeks' radiotherapy. Did you have that?

Maria: No, I had an operation and then chemotherapy. It was very scary when I first learned I had cancer, but you do get on with it, and once you start your treatment you could find, as I did, that you get used to the idea. At the group we've all been through the stage of being diagnosed, told you have cancer, and then having some sort of treatment. . . . Many people find it helps to talk to someone else who's had it.

Caller: Yes, I don't know what to tell the family. I have to be so strong for them. Do you know of anyone who has had treatment exactly like mine will be? [*crying*]

Maria: It's OK, take your time, we can talk for as long as you wish . . . there are other women in our group who have had radiotherapy and I can give you a phone number for one of them if you like. . . .
Caller: Someone's just come in. I'll have to go. Can I call you later to talk a bit more?
Maria: Of course, any time up to 10 tonight or again tomorrow.
Caller: Thank you Maria. My name's Susan.
Maria: Well, bye for now, Susan.
Susan: Goodbye and thanks. . . .

Here the caller is unsure of what she wants, but on hearing that the supporter has identified with her situation, in this case from her own experience, and knowing that there are also others in the group with whom she could have contact, the caller is able to talk a little more and to release some emotion which does not put off the supporter. With such a safe environment and a rapport established, it is likely that the caller will ring again when she is not going to be interrupted.

Befriending

Moving further along the spectrum and indeed at what might be considered the opposite end of the spectrum from advice giving, befriending is emotional support, given unconditionally, by one human being to another. There is no contract between the two people, no requirement to 'qualify' for the service, and it involves the extensive use of active listening skills and is the least directive form of telephone work. The caller is listened to, heard and encouraged to talk further if they wish. The Samaritans is the most well-known service which offers telephone befriending 24 hours a day, all year round, when the caller needs it. Strictly speaking, Samaritan befriending is the provision of emotional support without which the caller, or befriendee, may go on to become actively suicidal. It might not be necessary for the befriendee to be recognisably suicidal – indeed the person may be in a state such that, with the absence of emotional support it is likely they would become suicidal. The Samaritans organisation does not judge, prescribe, analyse or advise callers and is absolutely confidential. The caller can remain anonymous.

Samaritan Volunteer (SV): The Samaritans, can I help you?
Caller: I'm not really sure that I should be troubling you . . . you see, I'm not about to kill myself . . . but I just need to talk to someone. . . .

SV: That's OK, there's plenty of time. . . . Why not try talking to me?

Caller: I . . . I . . . I just don't know where to start . . . [*crying*]

[*SV, absorbing the silence, doubt and uncertainty, leaves the silence for some minutes.*]

SV: Well, let's try together to explore what might be going on. . . . Perhaps you can tell me what was in your mind immediately before you decided to pick up the phone?

And so on.

Here The Samaritan volunteer, or befriender, simply allows the befriendee time to think and talk. The silences may be long, but there is no pressure of time on the caller. Gently, the befriender will explore with the caller whatever the situation might be. The befriender goes at the pace of the befriendee, using empathy to support the caller and giving the caller permission to be as they are, acknowledging the feelings they have.

In all of these communications across the spectrum, a relationship will have to be established between the caller and the person answering the call if the essence of the call is to be effectively addressed. The skills needed to carry out any type of telephone work are fundamentally the same, with an emphasis being placed more strongly in some areas than in others according to the nature of the service offered and, within that, the nature of each call. Where counselling differs from the rest of these will be seen throughout this book. In any telephone situation, the worker must be appropriately trained in order to be able to move comfortably between *the service's specific parameters* for crisis intervention, support, information or advice giving as each call to the service requires.

Telephone helplines

All the examples above can be carried out successfully by people who are not trained counsellors and may be part of the work of a telephone helpline. The term 'telephone helpline' can therefore mean a telephone service which has an active listening and supportive focus, provides factual information or is a combination of any of these. Further, the helpline may be a short term service, such as those which are linked to a specific television or radio programme and can be available just for a few hours or a few days after the programme's transmission, or a long term, permanent service, such as the many helplines operated by health-focused charities, children's charities, employee assistance programmes and welfare groups. Helplines may be operated on a local level, such as those run by many self-help groups.

With most helplines, the calls are mainly 'one-offs'. Dealing with the fact that the caller may never be in touch again and may never come back to report on progress, action or even when things go wrong, can take much getting used to and can be quite hard for some people to accept. This is one area that is essential to address in supervision for those working on a helpline. Indeed, the likely lack of feedback from the caller, and the possible impact this can have, is often overlooked as part of training. It is interesting to note that helpline workers, even those experienced in the medium, sometimes fall into the trap of subliminally soliciting feedback on the phone with phrases such as 'I hope that's been useful' or 'I'm sure that you will find you can now do. . . .' It is too easy to put pressure on the caller to praise the call because of the worker's own need to be needed and valued – on hearing phrases like these the caller will invariably respond in the positive, giving the worker the instant gratification sought. If this is almost always the way a call is ended, some examination of the motives, level of satisfaction and personal needs of the worker and the worker's suitability to helpline work should be carried out.

There are also regular callers to a helpline who do seem to be progressing, however slowly, with each call, and who might easily call occasionally for a number of months. With some services, the helpline's arrangement is for a particular worker always to work with that regular caller. The process of this work could be similar to brief counselling although it should be more accurately labelled 'brief support work' since the helpline worker is not working as a trained counsellor. For brief work, the caller and worker do not formally agree a contract. Rather, the caller is likely to ring as the need arises and if the specific worker is not available may be told when to ring back to speak with that person, or they may be offered the opportunity to talk to whoever has answered the call. If a helpline does offer a caller the opportunity to speak to a specific helpline worker on a regular basis, they should consider including this specialist aspect in their training, since ongoing work is very different from one-off calls, even if the service is not offering formal counselling or therapy.

It is worth noting here that there is a big difference between regular callers who are 'working' and are using a telephone service as a support or prop or sounding board for their experiences and repeat callers who at their most destructive could be considered nuisance callers. These repeat callers might call and be difficult or abusive or might call because they are lonely or isolated and wish to talk . . . and talk – which might be considered an abuse of the service, preventing 'genuine' callers from reaching the service. All organisations must decide on what is considered an appropriate use of their service and respond to callers accordingly. If the service does not wish to be a listening ear for as long as and as often as a particular caller requires, then workers must be trained in challenging and preventing repeat callers from using the service. The distinction between appropriate callers and inappropriate callers can be made by asking: 'Who does this service seek to help, how and why?', followed by, 'For whom is this service inappropriate and why?' Training and techniques for excluding the latter category can then be given.

The Telephone Helplines Association (previously known as the Telephone Helplines Group) attempted to quantify the use of a range of helplines in 1993 by asking a variety of helplines to estimate the number of calls per month to their services. This rough calculation produced the astonishing result that in the UK at that time, a call was made to a helpline every seven seconds.

Whether trained counsellors or not, anyone seeking to work by telephone with vulnerable people or people in distress should have enough integrity to ensure that they provide a high quality service. In the booklet *Guidelines for Good Practice in Telephone Work* (Telephone Helplines Association, 1993), standards for good telephone helpline practice are suggested. These have been devised such that any organisation, large or small, should be able to follow their guiding principles.

Help by telephone is not limited to the world of charities and the voluntary sector. Commercial employee assistance programmes, for example, clearly generate revenue for the companies which run them and private counsellors charge for their telephone counselling work.

Preventing abuse of people using the telephone for support or counselling

All of the people mentioned so far in this chapter should be clearly abiding by codes of ethics and practice laid down by the British Association for Counselling (BAC), the Telephone Helplines Association and other professional bodies as appropriate for the service. Indeed, people seeking *counselling* by telephone are always well advised to check that this is so before commencing sessions.

Sadly, it cannot be ignored that the telephone is a potentially big cash-generating market place for help and support and in that capacity it can be open to abuse. There are always those who do not follow ethical codes and there have been situations in which people have set up so-called counselling helplines which then turn out to be a front for illegal activities. People have also set up and advertised private telephone counselling services charging premium call rates.

The Independent Committee for the Supervision of Standards of Telephone Information Services, known as ICSTIS, is a watchdog body which was established in September 1986 to supervise the content of, and the promotional material for, telephone services which operate under premium rate tariffs. It is funded by a levy on that industry and its primary task is to investigate public complaints relating to the content/promotion of premium rate services. It has a code of practice relating to the content and promotion of premium rate services, monitors services to ensure compliance and recommends measures to achieve compliance. Whilst on the subject of premium rate services, it is worth noting that the Telephone Helplines Association will not accept into membership any helpline organisation whose contact number for the public uses premium rate telephone charges.

It is to be hoped that genuine helplines, counselling organisations and individual counsellors can be recognised while those who are not operating within ethical codes can be prevented from using vulnerable people as a source of income.

As will be seen in more detail in Chapter 3, the BAC seems to be starting to accept the fact that counselling by telephone does exist in its own right and it is possible to envisage that counselling, such as is carried out by organisations, by individual counsellors or therapists quoted in some of the case studies in this book, *will* soon come to be fully recognised as a specialist area of counselling. This would be a specialist area for which there is additional, nationally and internationally recognised training after perhaps a basic counselling certificate, diploma or even degree. It then follows that one day with the inclusion of studying to gain a broad theoretical background, it *should* be possible to train and supervise specifically as a telephone counsellor.

2

Skills and Attitudes Needed when Counselling by Telephone

This chapter considers the specific counselling skills which are required when counselling by telephone. A number of books (such as Culley, 1990) consider counselling skills for the relative newcomer to face to face counselling, and many of the skills outlined here are similar. Of course, having the skills alone does not make for a good telephone counsellor. Aspects of personal and practical awareness, both of the individual counsellor and of organisations, with regard to telephone work are discussed, highlighting issues about the working conditions required.

Many of the skills that a counsellor requires in order to be effective exist right across the world of counselling. There is, however, a considerable difference in terms of the greater significance of some areas for counselling by telephone compared with individual face to face work: for example voice pitch and tone.

Carrying out counselling by telephone is similar to existing in a vacuum. The telephone connection between the counsellor and the client, and the relationship which subsequently results, is such that, for the duration of the session, it is like occupying a world totally separate from any other that either the counsellor or the client experiences. Immersed in a telephone counselling session, usually requiring the physical holding of the telephone handset, both people are isolated from anything extraneous as if enclosed in a bubble.

Some of what occurs in the telephone counselling setting is a matter of actually stating the obvious: those things which may be taken for granted by either party when a client and a counsellor are in the same room for a session. For example, it is easy to make assumptions about a client, whether or not these are later proved to be accurate, from the way the person is dressed, how they enter the room, how they sit. It is equally easy for the client to make similar assumptions about the counsellor. Indeed, I do not think it is possible to engage in any counselling relationship, face to face or on the telephone, without making assumptions, but it is essential for a counsellor to be aware of these and not to allow them to cloud or to block the counsellor's attentiveness.

In addition, when counselling by telephone, the lack of visual contact means that it is very easy to believe in all that the client says. It is not always easy to detect what might be a client's fantasy about any situation being talked about, because there is no physical way of reading the client's face or body language to provide supplementary clues that might contradict the words. One of the most difficult techniques to learn as a telephone counsellor is that of knowing when and how to challenge the suspicion of such a fantasy. Do it too soon and the client may well hang up. Leave it too long to challenge and it may be hard to distinguish between the fantasy and reality. The counsellor's own fantasies about the client must also be examined in supervision and are referred to later in this book. As the client–counsellor relationship develops over a few sessions, the counsellor should become aware of what is the usual telephone manner or behaviour for that client and so should find it easier to be aware of what is different, whether or not it is appropriate to challenge the client or to point out the perceived differences.

Assessment skills

Assessment skills are a very important part of telephone coun-selling, indeed perhaps *the* most important part of the work, particularly in one-off or shorter term counselling. McLennan et al. (1994) sought to compare telephone counsellors' conceptualising abilities and counselling skills to see whether accurate assess-ments of callers' needs were made and whether there was a correlation between the assessments and the counsellors' skills in responding to the clients' needs. Previous research by others had used external people to rate the counsellors' performances without any experimental control over the nature of the clients' problems. McLennan's concern was that this could lead those rating the counsellors to make judgements which could be very different from assessments made by the clients themselves.

Two studies were carried out. The first was concerned with the telephone counsellors' post-interview conceptualisations of callers' problems. The second used Kagan's (1976) Interpersonal Process Recall (IPR) which is a recall technique to study counsellor and client experiences in relation to the counselling process, in order to retrieve the counsellors' conceptualisations which were made during the course of their interviews. Actors were recruited to be 'clients' and were given scripted situations to play, created following consultation with experienced telephone counsellors.

In the first study, the 'clients' rated the way in which they experienced each counsellor on pre-determined score ranges, according to how accurately each counsellor identified the problem(s), the client's needs and the counsellor's overall accuracy. At the end of each call, the researcher asked the counsellor to explain what she or he had experienced to be the client's problem(s), the causes, and how best the counsellor believed the client could be further helped. Each interview was transcribed and was the basis for rating counsellor skill level and conceptualisation accuracy, using McLennan's Counsellor Response Quality Rating Scale (1990a). The content of each interview was also checked to ensure the client had been consistent with the script and each client rated her or his in-role reaction to the counsellor using McLennan's (1990b) Client Perception Measure.

In the second study, Kagan's IPR procedure was used after each interview to help the counsellors to recall their thoughts about the problems presented by the caller and the needs which the counsellors perceived and which then guided the way they responded during the call.

Among the conclusions were that the counsellors who had greater experience of telephone work, and who were actually more skilled telephone counsellors, were able to work with more, and varied, issues raised by the caller and did not jump in to offer information in one area only. They did not make snap assessments and then act on these alone. It was noted that each telephone counsellor's level of performance during a session was related to the accuracy with which the counsellor conceptualised the issues raised during the session, but was not related to general conceptualisations made after the session when a post-session interview was held between the counsellor and the researcher. Further, while the counsellors' performances were reasonably consistent with each of their calls, their level of accuracy of conceptualisation of the clients' (scripted) concerns varied widely.

This has implications for the training of telephone counselling skills, for it suggests that counsellors were clearly able to use their skills of active listening consistently, but did not seem always to adapt them in order to be able to address different clients' different needs. The counsellors' cognitive processes and their ability to assess accurately the nature and severity of the caller's problem was seen as being increasingly important in achieving a 'successful' outcome to the call *in the client's terms*.

Asking a counsellor at the end of a session how it went was found by McLennan to be less effective at linking the counsellors' conceptualisations with the actual responses made, than if their actual responses are fed back to them. This suggests that there is a case to be made for taping trainees, but if this is to be carried out by telephone it must be done in line with telecommunications regulations, as certain conditions would apply (see Chapter 7).

The study also indicates that Kagan's IPR can be extremely useful for enhancing trainee counsellors' cognitive processes and might be an effective tool as part of telephone counsellor supervision.

It is not then surprising to note that one of the suggestions made as a result of the study is that training courses need to focus on assessment skills to ensure that telephone clients get a better service. In so doing, it is not simply a case of being able to 'diagnose'; it is essential to be able to use the assessments in an interactive way with the client.

My experience in teaching telephone training courses and supervising helplines bears out McLennan's findings. The part of a telephone conversation leading to 'diagnosis' is quite easy, but the next step to interacting at the correct level and in the most suitable way for the *client* at that time can be far harder to get right, particularly with a client who raises many painful issues in a session. Why might this be? Perhaps it is harder to empathise and work with negativity when one cannot see the impact of one's words. The dynamics of the telephone client–counsellor relationship must have some impact on how difficult situations are handled, when compared with working in the same room as the client. Some of this may well be linked to the fact that it is easier for the telephone counsellor to get caught up in the great unknown of what happens next to the client after the session, than it is for the face to face counsellor, who might have had some reassurance perhaps from the physical, in-the-same-room contact during the session. This further stresses the importance of regular supervision for telephone counsellors.

The McLennan research illustrates how difficult it can be to assess clients accurately in telephone counselling. Apart from the counsellor assessing whether or not she or he is an appropriate person to be working with the client according to what the client is expressing, it is essential to establish, perhaps using more questioning than in face to face work, that the client is clear about the purpose of the sessions and can meet the counsellor's contractual requirements (see Chapter 5). In general face to face counselling, an assessment session, which might include taking notes of the client's history, allows for much to take place between the client and the counsellor; as much may be unsaid as is spoken, the counsellor taking great notice of body language, for example. How does this happen and what are the components of a successful telephone session?

The following are 12 essential considerations which might be employed during a one-off, an initial or an early session of skilled telephone counselling, where the client–counsellor relationship is not well established. In establishing a new client–counsellor relationship, the counsellor has to introduce the client into the counsellor's style of working, which may or may not include, for example, in-depth work with transference or working with setting goals.

Welcoming the client

The makings of a good relationship can be quickly established by phone. Similarly, there is a risk that these can also be quickly destroyed if the counsellor's tone, words, pattern of speech or accent are very different from what the client expects, for example if the greeting is too brisk. With a new client at the first session or at the preliminary session, the counsellor must be particularly aware of this and should listen acutely to how the client responds to the greeting and if necessary adapt language or tone. This is further discussed in the next section, but suffice to say that extra care and attention to the first few seconds of the call can make all the difference to the rest of the session(s).

Remember that most people do not really hear a name or organisation's title if it is the first thing given to them. When calling somewhere, especially for the first time and even more so if the caller is anxious about making the call, it takes several seconds for the caller to process several facts *before* the interaction takes place. These facts are:

(a) The phone is ringing and not engaged.
(b) There is no answerphone or electronic voice cutting in.
(c) 'I hope I've dialled the right number.'
(d) 'It is definitely ringing . . . what shall I say?'

This suggests that a hurriedly answered phone, quickly stated name and then a platitude like 'How can I help you?' can throw the caller off track. It means that the caller has to say something like 'Oh, is that _____?' to check they have indeed got the right person/organisation.

Instead, let the phone ring about three times before you answer it (which obviously means that you need to ensure that your answerphone will not cut in before you do pick up the call), then state the greeting word(s) first, then your name (or organisation's name), and then pause.

Listening and responding skills

Telephone counselling requires an interactive approach, far more than do many types of counselling or psychotherapy with client/patient and counsellor/therapist in the same room, even if in some cases both parties are not actually sitting looking at each other.

The listening and responding required for telephone counselling is far more intensive than that required for a general telephone conversation. With the absence of visual cues, a sighted counsellor will therefore need to develop extra listening skills for telephone work.

One of the most important areas in many aspects of counselling is the unsaid, so part of listening on the telephone will be to attend to what is not openly expressed. It may be necessary to ask more open questions and to reflect, paraphrase and summarise more than one would do in a face to face session, to check out what is going on for the client, while being careful not to push the client down a route of *the counsellor's* choosing.

The so-called minimal encouragers, or verbal gesturing – 'mmm', 'yes' , 'I see', 'go on', 'aha' and so on – are all needed to let the client know that the counsellor is still present at the end of the phone and has not become bored, fallen asleep or left the room.

It is essential to allow time for the client to finish thinking or deliberating without the counsellor jumping in to finish the sentence or imagined train of thought. In listening to silence, the counsellor should be alert to the last thing either party said as a means of providing possible clues to the reasons for the silence (see next section).

Of course the counsellor will also be listening to the actual words spoken, the slang or colloquialisms, the way phrases are connected and the pitch and tone of the client's voice. While one advantage of telephone counselling is that a counsellor can work with a client who is at the other end of the country, this in itself can bring new challenges in understanding with regard to dialect, accent and phrases used by both parties. Many dialects and accents can sound stronger over the phone and it should be the counsellor's responsibility to be aware of this possibility and to ask for clarification of phrases used. This makes it easier for the client to ask the counsellor in turn to explain things not fully understood. It is very easy to lose or confuse when talking on the telephone.

All of this will add to the counsellor's imagined picture of the client – and vice versa – and the counsellor must be wary of allowing a picture in the 'mind's eye' to compensate for the lack of face to face contact. It is vital to keep this in check and to respond to what is presented, checking out any assumptions, clarifying and exploring. It is essential that the 'mind's eye' does not become too dominant and interfere with the session.

There are times when the counsellor needs to interrupt the client and so should be aware of techniques for doing this. One way to silence or to focus an incessant telephone talker is to remain totally silent and not to respond to anything that is said. Although not instantly effective, it should not be too long before the person dries up or seeks encouragement to continue. An alternative way is simply to talk over the person until they stop talking. Neither of these techniques is easy to do for counsellors who aim to use empathy and to be a 'good listener', and they are not being recommended as general good telephone counselling practice for all counsellors, but might be useful occasionally. On the other hand, it is sometimes necessary to interrupt a client who seems to be confused, is getting tied up in knots, is sounding increasingly muddled, is going round in circles about whatever is being said, or is repeating themselves. It might require a definite interruption by the counsellor to cause the client to stop so that the counsellor can point out what seems to be going on and can help the client to re-focus: 'I can hear that there is a great deal you wish to say about this but I am finding I am getting muddled with all the information. Can we just go back to. . . .'

When there is background noise, the counsellor may need to take responsibility for addressing this. A closed question enables the client to give a straightforward, definite response: 'I have just heard what sounds like a door opening. Are you still able to talk with me?' Similarly, if there is noise in the counsellor's background it is essential that the counsellor reassure the client if it is still fine to continue to talk: 'You might be able to hear some noise in the background. There is no one actually able to hear what we are talking about and I am still giving you my complete attention.'

Clearly if the client and counsellor are in the same room, any reasons for silences or the client's physical movement may be visually obvious. Over the phone, the counsellor may need to be proactive in stating what can be heard.

Finally, the issue of how long to spend talking together should be addressed for any counselling session. In ongoing counselling this will be agreed when the contract is agreed (see Chapter 5). In a one-off counselling call, a clear ending must be agreed: 'It sounds as if there are many issues you would like to discuss. Perhaps we can talk for another 20 minutes and then see what options are open to us after that.'

Understanding silences

One of the most important differences between the listening skills employed in face to face work and on the phone is the way in which the counsellor works with silences. When there are silences, it may be necessary for the counsellor to break them in some way. Conversely, it could sometimes be necessary to leave them be. On the phone it is hard to know when a natural pause becomes a meaningful silence and even perhaps what the silence might be about. A 10-second silence can feel more like 30 seconds and a 30-second silence more like a few minutes. Even three seconds can feel a long time with no verbal interaction and no visual information.

Experience is the main factor which determines whether a counsellor will take action to break a silence – or not. How and when to challenge the silence, to explore it or to leave it until the client speaks requires confidence on the part of the counsellor. It is likely that the counsellor will find that in general there is a tendency to break silences more quickly when she or he is new to counselling by telephone. In addition, when any telephone counsellor is working with a new client there might be more of a need for the counsellor to break silences while the relationship is new and the counsellor is seeking to establish what some of the caller's concerns might be. Since there is no hard and fast rule about how long to wait before the counsellor breaks a silence, it will depend entirely on the individual client's natural style, on the counsellor's style and on how well established is that particular counselling relationship.

Silences may arise because the client is reflecting on something. This is usually a constructive part of the counselling process and can last for some seconds. As the sessions go on and both the client and counsellor become more comfortable with each other, these silences might be expected to increase in number or length without causing undue anxiety to either person. Some counselling techniques with an analytic base, however, require counsellors to leave silences for the client to break. This is probably not an appropriate way to work on the telephone as there are already too many potentially unnerving unknowns for the client, such as the assumptions or fantasies made about the counsellor and the counselling process, without having to introduce more potential causes of anxiety.

The telephone is an excellent medium for enabling the client to feel safe enough to reveal something without feeling too exposed or vulnerable. A silence might arise, however, if the client reveals something to the counsellor about which they have never before spoken. Wondering how the counsellor will have heard that and what the counsellor might be thinking about it could keep the client silent. Or the counsellor may have challenged the client and the client is angry and may prefer silence to expressing their anger at that time.

When the client is silent, all that the counsellor has to go on is what has already been said, particularly the last thing said before the silence and by whom it was said. By reflecting on the session so far, starting with the last thing said by both parties, since that is often the most likely trigger for the client's silence, the counsellor should be provided with a clue as to what the silence might be about.

Recognising and responding to feelings

If the client is distressed, it may sometimes be difficult for this to be clearly expressed. If there are no obvious clues such as crying or rage, how can a counsellor pick up on a client's feelings?

Listening for sighs, pauses, hesitations, when the subject is changed or when the client sounds vague are all clues to some distress or emotion. The tone and pitch of the client's voice might disclose otherwise unexpressed feelings. A raised or a quieter pitch, a staccato or a rushed tone would all indicate that the client is experiencing some feelings concerned with the matter being spoken about or connected to the interaction with the counsellor.

The client might refer to a situation in the third person rather than in the first person when distressed, as if to create a distance between the event being discussed and the client. Asking a client to 'own' statements can help the client to become more in touch with feelings about an experience or issue. For example 'people don't like it when my brother swears a lot' would become 'I get upset because my brother swears almost all the time', which is a clearer opening for further exploration.

The client who openly expresses emotion on the telephone may require a slightly different response. How does a counsellor offer the telephone equivalent of a tissue to a client who is sobbing? As a general rule, interrupting the flow of emotion will simply block the client, so a sobbing client generally should be left to cry, the counsellor reassuring the client that 'it's OK, take your time' and 'I'm here . . .' so that the client is aware that the counsellor is there in the background. Many clients, such as those brought up in a 'stiff upper lip' culture will become embarrassed by their display of emotion and tend to keep apologising for crying. Again, the counsellor's reassurance and unhurried approach will enable the client to release at least a little of the bottled-up emotion.

Rage can also appear far sooner on the telephone. Again the preferred technique would be to let the client express the rage until it is through. As with tears, it is important for the counsellor to reassure the client that it is OK to express the emotions and that the counsellor will wait. It is worth bearing in mind that the raging client might not hear the counsellor's first reassurance, but a calm counsellor will usually get through in the end. Sometimes the client will move between rage and tears and the counsellor must be able to move with the client. Some angry clients might seek to displace their anger on to the counsellor: 'It's all your fault. You never told me that if I did _____ this could happen.' A defensive counsellor will simply fuel the client's fire.

The client has the ultimate power on the telephone – that of terminating the call – yet even the most furious, blaming client will often hang on, seeking the counsellor's interaction in some way even though this may not be something the client is actively aware of wanting. It is essential, therefore, that the counsellor's interaction is constructive to the client. It is also essential for the counsellor to be aware both of any feelings which the client is projecting and of the counsellor's own reactions, real or imagined, to the situation being discussed. In order to ensure that her or his own reactions do not dominate the session, the counsellor must be aware of her or his tone and pitch of voice and of the words used in response to the client.

It is important that the counsellor is clear of her or his boundaries about dealing with clients who are offensive, abusive, threatening violence to themselves or to others or suicidal. It can be useful to build into the contract what constitutes behaviour that the counsellor will not tolerate (see Chapter 5). Sanders (1993) discusses some of the issues a counsellor might want to consider in these areas.

Although not scientifically proven, anecdotal evidence from telephone counselling services, where experienced face to face counsellors also work on the telephone, suggests that the release of a range of emotions often tends to occur at a far earlier stage in the telephone relationship than it does when a client is face to face with a counsellor. Further, in many cases, the emotion expressed can be far deeper than the client might display if sitting in the same room as the counsellor.

It is essential that any counsellor intending to work by telephone is experienced in detecting and working with a range of emotions and must be confident about addressing these by telephone. Anyone undertaking telephone counselling work should include in their training some cathartic techniques and should also undergo personal therapy to enhance their own personal awareness.

Working with transference and fantasy

Some understanding of transference and countertransference is helpful for any successful telephone counsellor, regardless of counselling orientation. This is defined further in Chapter 4. It has been emphasised already that the medium of the telephone lends itself to assumptions, judgements and projections of which the counsellor must be constantly aware. It is worth pointing out that since much telephone counselling is short term work, often goal-oriented, transference may be less likely to be overtly raised in the work, although it doubtless exists.

People have very different expectations of telephone counselling. Some clients may well expect the counsellor to be able to give them the 'right psychological advice' because the counsellor is viewed as an 'expert'. This perception may be due to a genuine misunderstanding of the nature of counselling, and the counsellor should be sensitive to this possibility.

A skilled telephone counsellor will also be aware of their own perceptions of the client's situation and will be careful to avoid adding their own views or feelings, continuing instead to work with the client's interpretations. It can be difficult to maintain an awareness of this when one has never met or seen the client and this highlights one of the biggest differences in counselling process between face to face and telephone work. Encouraging the client to ask questions of the counsellor, right at the beginning of the contract, as described in Chapter 5, can be helpful in avoiding some of these issues before they dominate or block the work.

Of course there is also the possibility that a counsellor can relate to the client as she or he did to a previous client and can project inaccurate impressions or make false assumptions. It is to be hoped that the counsellor's professional training and supervision will address this. Any client who does not feel heard or does not feel that the counsellor understands or empathises with

what they are talking about, or senses that they are being confused with someone else, is unlikely to stick with sessions for very
long.

There is a danger of this occurring when a counsellor works
with numerous clients, perhaps on a telephone counselling helpline. Here, it is possible to find several callers talking of similar
issues and it is essential that the counsellor differentiates between
all the callers, responding to each as an individual, unique and
distinct from anyone else. This might seem obvious, but anyone
who has worked on a busy, specialised helpline for a time will
appreciate that the theory can be far easier to state than the
practice can be to uphold. A volunteer working for a helpline
summed up how she tried to ensure that each caller was clearly
different in her mind: 'Each call is like starting with a blank piece
of paper. You have to listen and let the [caller's] voice do the
writing.'

Time keeping

Most counsellors can sense when time is drawing to a close in a
face to face session, but on the phone 50 minutes or an hour
might not seem to be that. Indeed, 10 minutes' in-depth work can
seem like five, whereas five minutes' circular conversation can
seem like 15! Time keeping is one of the key boundaries for this
medium and the counsellor might be surprised at how different
the time or session length feels in the early days of telephone
counselling when compared with face to face work.

Session endings can give rise to many difficulties or fantasies if
they are not handled carefully. Did the client think the counsellor
was hurrying the session to an end because the counsellor had
something better to do? Was the client boring the counsellor? In a
face to face setting, a client can see if the counsellor starts to
move or look at a clock or a watch. This gives a clue that the
session is perhaps drawing to a close even if the counsellor does
not actually say so at that time. As this cannot happen when
counselling on the telephone, it is very important to tell the client
when the session is drawing to a close, perhaps giving a five-
minute 'warning' and then a two-minute 'warning' and then even
a final minute if appropriate.

The length of each session will depend on the contract agreed
between the counsellor and client, but a 50-minute hour, which is

commonly used by many face to face counsellors, is a good length of time for work to be done in a telephone counselling session. Whatever the length is to be, it should be decided beforehand rather than allowing sessions to be open-ended.

In some respects, this time boundary is one of the key issues which differentiates telephone counselling from specific telephone support, telephone befriending or indeed many telephone helpline calls. Support and befriending services will generally give the caller as long as she or he wants. The Samaritans, for example, applies no time limit to the calls it receives, so a caller may take as long as she or he needs.

Many helplines, however, do have a limit of perhaps 20 or 30 minutes, beyond which it is argued that the majority of calls would become unproductive or circular, and indeed many cite an average of about 15 minutes' call length. This is linked to the fact that helpline calls are very often 'one-offs', seeking perhaps to empower the caller to take action or to provide information and time for discussion. It is not expected that the worker will ever speak to that caller again, although this does sometimes happen.

Some counsellors argue that single session therapy can take place on the phone as it can face to face. This may be true if it is promoted as such and its boundaries are clearly explained to the client. Essentially telephone counselling, which is usually an ongoing, developing relationship, must have clear parameters, such as the length of a session from the outset, to establish the framework within which the counselling can occur.

The development of the relationship

At the start of this chapter, the concept of the relationship between counsellor and client as being in a vacuum was mentioned. The physical act of holding a telephone handset and concentrating totally on the conversation, without making copious notes or being interrupted by external distractions, increases the intensity of the contact. This raises a somewhat paradoxical intimacy. On the phone both parties are, in a sense, literally mouth to mouth in a way that they can never be in face to face counselling.

Although most clients and many counsellors are likely to use a telephone with a handset, it is of course possible to have headphone attachments or hands-free facilities on some phones.

Beware of hands-free facilities though! They can sometimes sound as if the speaker is in an echo chamber, which can be very off-putting. Further, any slight movement of the speaker's head away from the microphone may be detected and perhaps misinterpreted as the speaker moving away, losing interest, being distracted and so on.

The skill of hearing the unsaid and being aware of oneself, to ensure that there is checking out of one's projections and assumptions, builds on the relationship's intensity. All attention is devoted to the telephone and the person at the other end of the connection.

It is often possible to say difficult things on the phone, because one can concentrate on oneself and not have to see, and so be immediately affected by, the reaction (real or imagined) of the other person. With this level of attention and focus, it is inevitable that the two people are drawn closely together within a short time of entering into the relationship. Indeed the bond of trust between a client and a telephone counsellor can exist from the first session.

How easy it is to slip into assumptions, judgements and projections has already been mentioned, but a key issue for the development of the client–counsellor relationship is that of the client feeling valued. There may be a greater need on the phone for the client to hear encouragement or for the counsellor to be aware of anything they might inadvertently say which could be interpreted as rejection.

Confidentiality

The question of when, if ever, the counsellor may breach confidentiality must be made very clear to all clients, for it is important that the client is aware of this possibility. All telephone counsellors must have a sense of what for them might constitute such action and why (see Chapter 5). Bond (1993) provides guidance about standards and ethics for counsellors.

One occasion concerning confidentiality, which is often raised at helpline counselling skills training sessions, is the question of how to deal with a telephone client who expresses suicidal feelings. A counsellor might have been trained, perhaps as a Samaritan, to talk with suicidal clients, or might have a long-established relationship with the client which would perhaps guide the counsellor's behaviour in line with any procedures. If neither of these is the case, it might be appropriate to ask the client what they would like you to do: whether to stay on the line and talk or to call someone to help the client. Clarke and Fawcett (1992) reviewed risk factors for evaluating someone who might be suicidal and described a 10-step process for detecting and gauging suicidal attitude. All counsellors should be aware of the possibility of a client becoming suicidal. This is an area of work which can easily raise anxieties for some counsellors and should be checked out during supervision. As a holding measure and in practice, counsellors can and do refer their clients to The Samaritans.

Exactly what action might be taken is dependent on the individual counsellor's own experience, supervision and contract and confidentiality guidelines if working alone in private practice; any action which might constitute a breach of confidentiality must be covered by clear guidelines and procedures established by any organisation operating a telephone service. In addition, the impact of telecommunications technology on the confidentiality of the relationship should not be overlooked (see Chapter 7).

Personal and social skills

The tone of voice the counsellor uses when answering the phone initially, the answerphone message if appropriate, the pitch and speed of talking, the counsellor's accent and the words used will quickly convey an impression to the client.

Imagine overhearing anyone with whom one is familiar talking on the phone. Even if one does not know to whom the person is talking, it is often possible to determine whether or not they are talking to a close friend, an acquaintance, a child or a business or professional contact, from the language used, tone of voice, expressions of emotion and so on.

For telephone counselling, a warm, friendly manner is essential in order to offer a welcome. If the counsellor feels tired or under pressure, this will be subliminally taken in by the client. I do not believe that it is ever possible for a counsellor to conceal tiredness, boredom, anger, irritation or distraction from a client on the phone. Similarly, if the counsellor sounds too jolly, too friendly, too 'posh', too 'common' or too eager, the client might be put off. Some counsellors have a 'professional' voice which may be soft or low or which tends not to exhibit emotion on any level. It may be possible to get along fine with this voice with clients one sees, but on the telephone some signs of life and energy are essential. It can seem false at first to inject energy into one's speech – indeed, if overdone it can sound like the sugary sweet welcome heard as the kind of greeting received when making a telephone call to some commercial or public companies – but a little practice should develop an appropriately up-beat, professional counselling tone. For the counsellor who operates within a person-centred tradition where the need to be consistently genuine is important, there is some need to be aware of the issue of voice projection.

During a session, the slightest change in the counsellor's voice quality or tone will be detected, whether or not the client is 'brave enough' to openly state what they pick up.

In addition, the accent and the actual words the counsellor uses will create an impression on the client. Perhaps the counsellor is using jargon without checking that it is clearly understood, or perhaps the counsellor is oversimplifying words for the client. Finding the right balance without any visual clues to confirm or correct is quite a skill in itself. Asking the client 'Is that clear?' will not necessarily elicit a negative response – many clients are anxious about not upsetting their counsellor or appearing to be 'stupid' by admitting that they do not understand what is being said.

Working conditions

When working from home, if another member of the counsellor's household answers the phone, this might affect the client's perceptions and fantasies. There is also an issue to be taken into account: that of a counsellor who works from home 'training' other residents of all ages in how to answer the phone and not to interrogate the caller who could be a client. Ideally, to ensure good, professional practice, the counsellor working from home should have a separate telephone line and number, located in the room where the counselling takes place. This could be attached to an answerphone to eliminate the need for other members of the household to have to answer the line.

If there is much background noise during a session a client might be put off. Some people use telephones that have headsets rather than handsets. This certainly helps to block out external distractions, but the most important factor is that the counsellor must be in a quiet room, alone and undisturbed, if working from home. This also means the counsellor having the same discipline one might expect if working face to face, so that if the doorbell rings or some other interruption occurs, the counsellor's priority is the client and the session is not disturbed.

If working in an office, the ideal situation is to be alone or at least to be in a booth or partitioned-off area, again with headsets to reduce background noise. Others must be informed and understand that they should not interrupt if the counsellor is on the telephone, however significant they think their interruption is.

It is important to acknowledge how tiring or draining a single telephone session can be, reflecting the intensity of working in this medium. The counsellor must allow time for a walk around, a debrief of some sort and a break before another client's session. The typical 'therapeutic' 10-minute break may not always be sufficient, and having more than two telephone clients 'back to back' can be exhausting. Indeed, it would be unsustainable to have more than four telephone counselling clients in any one day. Certainly working at this pace for more than three days a week would be quite unhealthy in the long term.

Taking notes

The issue of note taking can stir up controversy and a range of opinions like almost no other. This means that people who would usually doodle while holding telephone conversations might need to refrain while working in a telephone counselling setting.

Experienced helpline workers report that distressed callers often have extremely acute hearing, to the extent that the sound of a pen moving across a paper can be detected. For some callers this can heighten anxiety: 'Why are you writing things down? What will you do with the notes?' 'I thought this was a confidential service.' Incidentally, it also seems that the more confident and experienced helpline workers are, the fewer notes they tend to take, mainly relying on and trusting to their ears, their listening skills and their instincts for the duration of the call.

The issue of keeping notes and records with regard to confidentiality needs to be clear, but one way of off-loading from the session is to jot notes about it as soon as it is over, whether these are kept for supervision purposes or immediately destroyed. Notes written up after the call as a personal debrief can also be reviewed after several sessions to see themes or patterns which might not have been obvious in the most recent session. Since many face to face counsellors do not take notes during sessions, why should the phone be any different? Copious note taking certainly affects the concentration and the client will, sooner or later, pick up on this. Sanders (1993) considers note taking and record keeping in relation to telephone work.

It is important to bear in mind data protection and regulatory issues with regard to keeping records or notes about clients and sessions. Organisations which have reason to store information about clients on computer, for example, must be registered under the Data Protection Act (see also Chapter 7).

Awareness

Awareness of projection and transference and the possible impact of these on the sessions, together with an awareness of personal working conditions, have already been mentioned in this chapter. Counselling by telephone challenges the traditional counsellor–client power relationship. The client has ultimate control during a telephone session, which cannot be said to be true of many face to face sessions.

There are other aspects of awareness which warrant special mention. Some counsellors make appointments directly with their clients by phone for their face to face work. Think of the impressions created in the briefest exchange of this type. Then think of how accurate they are when compared to the first face to face meeting, even with the benefit of having taken down certain personal details or having asked certain questions during the telephone conversation.

Think of one of your face to face clients. Go back over sessions you have had. What part do the non-verbal cues play in the sessions? How much notice do you take of hand movements, body language, clothes and general appearance? Is there ever conflict between the words spoken and the non-verbal gestures? What do you do if there is? Do you respond to this, pointing out the discrepancy to the client, or do you note it silently?

On the telephone, a counsellor obviously has to work without the guidance of visual clues. Some counsellors find it stimulating to 'learn' how to hear more acutely and find that not only do they enjoy telephone work, but also that their face to face practice benefits from their enhanced listening skills. On the other hand, the fact is that for some counsellors, telephone counselling holds too many uncertainties and unknowns for it to be satisfying.

Occasionally a counsellor and client may find that they literally cannot understand each other's words/mode of speech, in which case it must be the responsibility of the counsellor to point out what is happening and perhaps suggest alternative sources of help for the client.

Some counselling establishments operate within principles of equal opportunities, which counsellors are required to agree to follow. There should be guidelines and training on tackling client behaviour which contravenes the equal opportunities principles, whether the client is a face to face or a telephone client. Every counsellor working alone will have to decide for themselves what might be offensive to them, such as a client making racist statements or swearing profusely. The counsellor must be clear about her or his views and feelings and dealing with these, as well as being clear about if and how to challenge the client in this situation, which might require specific, additional training and practice.

Counsellors might not be at their ease with a client who wishes to talk about certain issues. One example of this is in the area of sexuality and sexual practices. Anne L. Horton (1995) considers how some telephone workers' own ignorance, embarrassment or unresolved transference/countertransference issues around sex and sexuality can lead to clients feeling rejected and discouraged from seeking further help. Either the counsellor's or the client's religious beliefs, attitudes towards disability, or towards older people or young people, to name but a few further examples, can also influence whether or not the client and counsellor are able to work effectively together.

Summary for setting up good telephone practice

A telephone service is often viewed by those who have little experience of such work as a cheap option: 'All you need is a phone and a person to answer it.' In other words, the telephone work is simply an 'add-on' to other work.

Guidelines for Good Practice in Telephone Work (Telephone Helplines Association, 1993) contains sections which cover, among others, the management of the service, training, support and supervision of workers and confidentiality, and it suggests areas for consideration by anyone setting up a telephone service. Clearly then, operating a high quality telephone service cannot be achieved as an 'add-on'. Although the booklet was written for helplines rather than individual practitioners or counselling services, the principles are adaptable and applicable even to the lone counsellor.

Let's now consider the implications of setting up a telephone counselling service more fully. For a start, the organisation or individual should be very clear about what the service will seek to do. Who will be the clients or what sorts of issues is it appropriate to address? Any existing organisational policies and practices or personal counsellors' practices, with regard to confidentiality for example, may need to be amended to incorporate specific issues which the telephone work might present. It is important that an additional telephone line is installed with a separate number from the rest of an organisation's telephone lines. This reduces the chances of calls being inappropriately received by others in the organisation. Similarly, for the individual counsellor working from home, a separate line can be a distinct advantage as a means of ensuring that only the counsellor answers that particular telephone, which should be located in a suitable room where counselling sessions can take place.

Then it must be ensured that anyone who is working as a *telephone counsellor* receives some training in telephone counselling techniques regardless of their years of experience or expertise in face to face counselling (see Chapter 3).

If the counsellors are current employees or volunteers, consideration must be made of which tasks they will be relieved in order to be able to give a good service by phone, and they will need to be provided with regular support on an informal basis and regular supervision for the telephone counselling work they do. Note that there is mention of people and not just one telephone worker. In an organisational setting, it is essential that there are at least two people working for the service on any shift/ time when the counselling line is open, so that they can support each other and can share the pressure of delivering a consistent in-depth counselling service.

Finally, a thorough evaluation of the service offered by an organisation should be conducted after a year or more of operation and this should incorporate a review of all of its aspects to consider the quality of the service provided (see Chapter 3). The individual telephone counsellor, of course, should be regularly monitored through supervision and does not (yet) have to have her or his practice evaluated by anyone else, although as will be seen later in this book, two initiatives might change this. The first is the advent of National Vocational Qualifications for Telephone Counselling, and the second is that the British Association for Counselling has started to consider the criteria for the accreditation of counsellors working by telephone.

Summary of counsellors' skills for a counselling session early in a counselling relationship

While the skills should be familiar, using them for the telephone requires an awareness of the process of a telephone interaction:

1. Let the phone ring three times before you answer it. This enables both of you to prepare to talk.
2. Make sure that your greeting is brief and clear, starting with 'Hello' and then your name, or 'Good morning/evening' and then your name, which lets the caller know that they have dialled the right number and got the right person.
3. Then stay silent, so that by the time you have stated your name, the caller may say something like 'Hello, I wonder if you can help me. . . . I'm not really sure where to start.' Then you are into the session.
4. Use open questions, reflection and verbal gesturing to enable the client to talk as much as they want to in the early part of the session.
5. Once you are beginning to get a hint of some of the issues or alternatively if you are getting confused or overwhelmed by all that is being talked about, start to clarify using paraphrasing and summarising. Beware of being too directive on the phone and of inhibiting the client from being able to challenge you if you are not correct. To avoid this, preface your statements with 'I'm not sure, but it sounds as if . . ./seems to me. . . .'
6. Then stay silent to give the client a chance to think about what you have said and to go back and further clarify, change what was said or move on.
7. If in doubt, be honest! 'I'm not sure I understand what you mean by _____'
8. If you do not understand an accent, expression or situation that is being talked about, ask the client either to repeat what they have just said or to clarify it for you. 'Would you mind just telling me again about . . . as I didn't catch all of what you said', or 'Would you mind explaining to me what _____ is?'

9. Check out what might be going on in your 'mind's eye' to separate fact from fantasy: 'I'm beginning to get a sense of. . . . How does that sound to you?'

10. If it is hard to interrupt, stop hearing what the client is saying and concentrate on listening for when the client pauses for breath. As soon as you detect a pause, jump in with something like 'It seems to me that we've been over this before and I'm getting quite confused because it sounds a bit different this time/we're not really getting any clearer.'

11. Then take responsibility for picking up on one aspect which you perceive to be significant and suggest that as a tentative opener: 'Would you mind taking me back over _____?'

12. Take your next cue from the client. The client will quickly brush this aside and change course if you haven't picked up the most important thing, so go with this, interrupting for clarification when or if you need to.

13. If you hear background noise, be proactive in enabling the client to tell you if they can't talk freely. Use a closed question to help the client to answer you easily: 'I can hear something in the background. Are you unable to speak at the moment?' The answer to that can then lead to a decision to wait, to continue or to end and call again at another pre-arranged time.

14. When there is a silence, your first action should be to say nothing! Think about the last interaction that took place between you, who spoke last, what about, and so on.

15. After a few seconds, if you were the last to speak: 'It seems that my saying _____ has stopped our session, and I'm wondering why this might be?'

16. If you are in doubt about the reason for a silence, and the client does not break it, there is no harm in doing so: say perhaps 'I am wondering what this silence is about. . . .'

17. If the client is expressing any emotion or suddenly changes pitch or tone, listen! Hear what is going on behind the words, taking clues from the voice, the silences, the phrases.

18. Empathise with the situation: 'It sounds as if that could be very hard to do.'

19. And with the emotion: 'It feels to me as though there is such sadness around. . . .'

20. If the client is very distressed, angry or crying, say nothing substantial which could interrupt the flow of emotion. Wait for a pause before empathising.

21. Above all else, at all times make sure that your voice is calm, gentle and reassuring. It is important that the client is aware that you can withstand the emotion being thrown down the line without getting flustered or reacting to it in an unhelpful manner.

22. Do not be too definite if checking out transference issues or projections. It is far less threatening to the client to hear 'I'm not

sure [if I've got this right], but from what you've told me, it sounds as if you might be responding to me as you used to respond to your father. . . .'

23. If the end of the session is near, remind the client 'We've been talking now for 40 minutes, so we have just 10 more minutes left today. . . .'

24. If you do not have a fixed time limit but the client is simply repeating what has gone before, or you feel that the session should be drawing to a close because the time is running out, you could introduce this with a summary of your perceptions of what has been discussed and give some space for any final thoughts this might then invoke in the client before ending: 'We've talked about _____ and _____ and from what you've been saying it sounds as if _____ might be something to try one day. As we are going to have to end in 3 minutes, I wonder if there is anything else which you want to raise today [*pause*]?'

25. Finally: 'Well we can talk further about that next session if you wish, but we have to end now. . . .'

3

Training, Supervision and Quality Control

As far back as 1986, Sandra L. Fish spoke in America about crisis line communication as a form of mediated therapeutic communication, based on 'the existence of a crisis and the medium of the telephone which shapes the intervention'. She went on to say that effective crisis counselling required specific communication skills carried out within the framework of a crisis intervention model. Some of the areas she defined as important for successful work in this way are those of the recruitment and training of therapists/counsellors, the use of counselling, the environment in which the counselling takes place and the policies within which the service operates. The therapist/counsellor's qualities needed for working on the telephone with a client in crisis must include sensitivity, stability, compassion, caring and a relaxed manner.

Fish's paper discussed the four stages of a crisis situation as defined by Brockopp in 1973:

1. The individual [sufferer] responds to the critical situation by employing her/his usual problem-solving methods with increased activity.
2. Having been unsuccessful in the attempt, the person experiences an increase in tension, disorganisation and disequilibrium.
3. The individual draws on additional resources, both external and internal, leading to successful resolution or diminution of the problem.
4. If the problem remains, the individual may move to more drastic attempts at resolution including complete withdrawal or isolation, suicide or psychosis.

A person in crisis may reach out at any stage of the process and the therapist/counsellor's response will differ depending on the stage of the crisis. There are several forms of support to be offered to an individual experiencing any form of life stress. The telephone can be an easy medium to access in a stressful time and at any stage of the crisis.

That was the view by a practitioner in the US ten years ago. It still holds true today. To work with people in crisis, or indeed with people who may not be in crisis but who wish to look at and explore aspects of themselves and their lives in some way, the telephone offers a viable alternative to face to face work. As with any other aspect of counselling, training, supervision and experience are vital components for practice and success (see also Fish and Gumpet, 1990).

In this chapter, training and supervision will be discussed together with issues of quality control and evaluation.

How does a counsellor develop the skills for counselling by telephone?

Training and accreditation

This book has made one big assumption: that all those intending to provide counselling by telephone are already fully trained face to face counsellors first, because there is no equivalent training or qualification solely in *counselling* by telephone in 1996. There are many courses which offer *telephone counselling skills* but this is not the same thing, as will be made clear below.

The Accreditation and Recognition Committee of the British Association for Counselling formed a working group which met three times during early 1996 to clarify where counselling by telephone fits within the BAC accreditation process. The group reported back to the Accreditation and Recognition Committee in May 1996. Although more work is still to be done, at the time of writing there are some clear criteria which, it is to be hoped, will clarify the basis of assessing counselling by telephone and its inclusion alongside face to face work for accreditation as well as perhaps one day standing alone for specific accreditation. If this work can proceed, formal, recognised training for telephone counsellors might follow along the lines of the requirements for accreditation.

This book has stated that there is a difference (as well as similarities and overlap) between using counselling skills to work on the telephone – as do most helplines, where, it must be remembered, workers are not operating in the capacity of trained counsellors (whether or not they have undergone such training) – and offering formal counselling by telephone. *Counselling skills* telephone work requires active listening, the use of open questions, paraphrasing and summarising and, of course, empathy. All of these will be familiar to anyone who has read of Egan's Three Stage Helping Model (Egan, 1990). *Counselling by telephone* requires all of these skills, as well as an understanding of negotiating a contract and an understanding of the counselling process, which may include working with fantasy or projection, an awareness of problem-solving strategies and an appreciation of a variety of counselling and therapeutic models leading to an integrated approach. Counselling by telephone must include a high level of personal awareness and of one's personal prejudices, and a willingness to commit oneself to, and work within, an ongoing relationship. Further, training for telephone counsellors should pay some attention to the counsellor's voice. Skilled application of tone and pitch and the use of pauses will be needed. One way of trying out some variations is to ask: how does the voice sound to the counsellor if the counsellor closes her or his eyes? Or if the counsellor makes a tape recording of her or his voice and then plays it back? The importance of the voice and what it can convey is discussed in Chapter 5.

In the training of telephone counsellors some reference should be made to single-session therapy and to shorter term focused approaches to counselling to enable effective work to take place even in one-off sessions. Talmon (1990) believes that some clients can be helped and empowered considerably by a single session of therapy. This is endorsed anecdotally from a non-therapeutic perspective by experienced helpline workers (not counsellors). In talking to people when gathering information for this book, I found that many confirmed my own experience that callers can seem to move on emotionally during the course of just one call, which might be considerably less than an hour in length (20 minutes seems to be an average call length for many helplines which offer 'emotional support' by telephone). For some callers the impact of the call is that they have been given an opportunity, perhaps the first ever, to explore or to clarify a situation or an experience, often anonymously and therefore 'safely'. It is not then so difficult to appreciate that a clearly structured single counselling/therapy session could achieve much with some clients.

National Vocational Qualifications

Having obtained a counselling qualification and with some experience of helpline work, it is now possible to work towards specific National Vocational Qualifications (NVQs) and Scottish Vocational Qualifications (SVQs) in telephone counselling.

Standards considered applicable to both face to face and telephone counselling work are laid out in the published standards as eight separate 'A' units. These cover functions common to the whole of the Advice, Guidance, Counselling and Psychotherapy Lead Body's (1995) remit and include areas such as 'Establish contact with clients', 'Develop and maintain interaction with clients', 'Evaluate and develop own work' and 'Operate referral procedures'. There are also 'B' units, of which there are 13, which cover specialist competencies and are not therefore commonly applicable. These include 'Assist clients to decide on options for meeting their requirements', 'Provide support for clients in planning a course of action', 'Ensure a structured counselling setting', 'Develop the counselling relationship' and 'Monitor self within the counselling process'.

At the time of writing, suites of qualifications for telephone counselling had not been finally decided. These are the combinations of standards which make up an NVQ or SVQ. It is important for anyone interested in pursuing this to check the current position at the time of application. Whatever the case, to obtain an NVQ or SVQ in Telephone Counselling will require demonstration that both 'A' units and 'B' units, including the specific telephone unit, are carried out in practice.

The single category within the 'B' unit standards which is quite specific to telephone work is called 'Working with the caller on the phone'. This has its focus on the telephone counselling process and covers the following areas:

Establish and develop contact with callers   This includes the way in which the telephone is answered by the counsellor, paying attention to the tone and pitch of the caller's (client's) voice, the caller's circumstances and situation, the way in which trust is established in the early part of the call, and how the nature of the call is assessed, including its appropriateness for that counsellor or organisation. It also addresses the skills required of the counsellor in order to fulfil all of these.

Sustain interaction with callers   Here the emphasis is on the ongoing call and enabling the caller to talk and explore issues through good telephone skills and awareness. The counsellor's intonation, use of silences and of supportive 'mmms' (verbal gesturing) as well as the more obvious skills of paraphrasing, active listening, empathy and perceptiveness and awareness of the client's experience are all to be measured.

Use telephone medium to the benefit of callers   This addresses issues of confidentiality, accessibility of the service, the immediacy of the telephone and the ways in which the caller is facilitated to share concerns. It also covers contracting issues in terms of working together to benefit the caller.

A number of issues within each of these categories address ethical codes, equal opportunities practice, the need for clearly laid down boundaries of the service available and procedural documentation to support the practice.

The fact that standards now exist specifically for telephone counselling within the NVQs is a positive step that recognises the value of the medium and practice.

Counselling children on the phone

This is a specialised area in its own right. The training any counsellor needs, in addition to their past experience of counselling and telephone work, in order to move successfully to work in this area is not to be underestimated. Yet, just as with telephone counselling for adults, there are currently no nationally recognised qualifications in this. Hereward Harrison, Director of Children's Services at ChildLine, explains that for a person to receive a ChildLine 'in-house' certificate, 75 hours of satisfactory, closely supervised, telephone work must have been achieved in addition to the 40 hours or so of initial training. Supervision and training then continue regularly after this point and the individual is considered as having achieved the minimum requirements to work with the children and young people who phone ChildLine.

Kids Help Foundation is a non-profit fundraising organisation dedicated to the health and well-being of Canadian children. It launched Kids Help Phone in 1989. This is a bi-lingual, confidential helpline that enables young people to talk to professional counsellors, toll free, 24 hours a day. All the telephone counsellors at Kids Help Phone are trained professionals and the service provides assessment, emotional support, brief therapy, information and referrals to local services. For life-threatening situations, the service offers crisis intervention and the mobilisation of emergency response services.

Its handbook clarifies what young people expect from telephone counselling as well as going through the fundamental skills the counsellor needs in order to enable the young person to talk and to work with the counsellor. Further, the book makes suggestions about what counsellors need to do to take care of themselves. Although the telephone counselling service can be used alone by young people who are not needing, seeking or receiving other assistance, the agency also sees itself as an extra service to help young people such as those who are already receiving face to face counselling, who are in child protection settings, or in mental health centres.

The model of helping operated by Kids Help Phone is based on principles from several theoretical models. The handbook (1994) talks, for example, of making contact with a caller, engaging the caller, clarifying the issue, developing solutions and terminating the call. The service offers the greatest degree of accessibility possible: it is free and allows callers to remain anonymous. Among the ways in which it defines its operation in the handbook are that it considers that all problems are 'legitimate' and acknowledges that it takes courage to call, whatever the reason. Callers initiate the process by making the call and determine what and how much they want to say. Counsellors help guide a caller towards a solution or resolution of the problem that initiated the call but the counsellor cannot solve the caller's problems. Callers and counsellors never meet face to face and personal information about counsellors is never revealed.

The handbook also acknowledges that all callers have problems, but not all problems can be dealt with effectively through a telephone counselling service. However, callers deserve the counsellor's full attention at all times and must receive consistent responses from counsellors. Consistency is achieved through training, supervision and peer support.

Some of the above might seem like common sense, but it is important that they are clearly stated to avoid assumptions being made or false expectations raised. They are equally applicable to telephone counselling services in the UK, and some of these areas are explored further elsewhere in this book.

Supervision for telephone counselling

It may be necessary to find a different supervisor from your face to face supervisor if you also work by phone. The supervisor needs to have an appreciation of telephone work as well as any particular counselling orientation used in order to be able to work most effectively. Indeed, it is appropriate to have some, if not all, supervision sessions by phone in order to experience the same medium as the client. If the telephone is used for supervision, a counsellor can choose a supervisor who does not live nearby, just as a client might derive benefit from being able to choose a counsellor for reasons which do not have to include geographical location. As with any counselling supervision, sessions must be regular, whichever medium is used.

The speed with which the client–counsellor relationship forms has already been mentioned and the implications of this for the supervisory relationship should be taken into account. It seems that a telephone client will place trust in the counsellor and will talk in greater depth far more quickly than if the client and counsellor were meeting physically in the same room each week. A supervisor has to have an understanding of this and to be able to adapt to this telephone process in order to be most effective for the counsellor. (See also Waters and Finn, 1995.)

As has been mentioned, it is harder on the telephone to be clear about the client's circumstances – a counsellor can work only with what the client chooses to tell and what the counsellor can hear in the background; any sound needs to be checked out and not assumed. As body language is not available to guide the counsellor, one must be careful to ensure that supervision does not become embroiled in supposition or fantasy. Rather than speculate, the supervisor can simply ask!

Case Study A
Supervision by telephone

*Annie is an experienced therapist and supervisor, who uses the
telephone extensively in different aspects of her work. Annie,
currently training to be a process-oriented psychologist (see
Chapter 4), has her own therapy and supervision by telephone.*

*When working as a supervisor herself, Annie's telephone
supervision is structured along the same lines as her face to face
work. This means that the person being supervised (whom I shall
refer to as the supervisee) pre-books the date and duration of the
next supervision session at the end of their current session. Most
sessions are an hour long, although occasionally an hour and a
half might be booked. The intensity of working by telephone leads
Annie to believe that an hour is really the optimum length for a
supervision session.*

*The supervisee is required to pay by cheque immediately after
the session. When agreeing a contract for supervision the supervisee is told that payment should be made following the session so
that it arrives with Annie within a few days of the session having
taken place. Annie charges the same fee for telephone supervision
as for face to face supervision. The telephone supervisee calls her
at the appointed time, so also pays for the cost of the phone call.
The face to face supervisee would, of course, pay travelling
expenses on top of the fee.*

*Annie believes that so much can be picked up by voice tone,
hesitations and the unsaid: she finds no reason why her work
cannot be carried out by telephone rather than face to face or in
combination with face to face work. In considering whether
differences might exist between telephone and face to face supervision sessions conducted with the same supervisee, Annie thinks
that there are no differences in the range, depth or style of work.
The key difference is that their work together is 'restricted to
relating, gathering information and communicating through the
auditory channel of experience alone'. Annie is aware that this
provides her with a greater sense of focus which is due to the tight
focus of the medium. Since Annie believes that all information,
both conscious and unconscious, is present or can be found in
speech, silence or other sounds, provided that one has the appropriate skills to uncover it, the telephone does not inhibit or prevent
the supervisor/supervisee relationship from working effectively.*

When Annie began to notice that she was enjoying telephone work more than face to face work, she explored why this might be the case. She discovered that she was not bringing her whole self into the face to face work since some of her energy was expended in trying to look like 'an adapted human being'. She was responding to an unconscious pressure to be what might be considered 'appropriate' or 'conventional' for a therapist or supervisor in a traditionally accepted manner. An example of this might be the way the therapist 'controls' her or his body language in the client's presence. Once she had recognised this, Annie started work with this in herself in order to be able to enjoy the face to face work as much as the telephone. So, for Annie, her work by telephone has modified and enhanced her face to face practice.

In terms of financial cost, there might be very little difference between being a telephone supervisee or a face to face supervisee. In terms of time, the costs of face to face supervision are greater, since the supervisee has to include travelling time to and from the session. On balance, I believe that telephone supervision is efficient and effective and provides a counsellor or therapist with a far wider pool of supervisors from which to choose. Practitioners are be able to select the supervisor most appropriate for their needs rather than having to introduce a geographical limiting factor.

I believe that it is also possible to have supervision groups by telephone. Using teleconferencing facilities, several people can be linked together for an agreed period of time, and case work can be considered. Group work by phone is discussed further in Chapter 6.

Support for telephone counsellors

How this is different from supervision varies according to the context in which the telephone counselling takes place. Working as part of a counselling team, for instance, support might be defined as the immediate off-loading to a colleague or a supervisor following a stressful session; it simply seeks to help the counsellor to unburden so that she or he can continue to work. In this setting, supervision would be a formally arranged, regular meeting, perhaps in a group format with some or all of the other counsellors and with a trained counselling supervisor. So the support is simply an opportunity for the counsellor to debrief, whereas the supervision would delve more deeply into certain sessions or aspects of sessions to consider the counsellor–client interaction and the therapeutic processes which occur, to gain insight into the client's situation and to consider ways of further helping the client.

If working as a lone telephone counsellor, then supervision will be regular and as described in the previous section. It is likely that support in this situation will take the form of note making after a session, a period of quiet reflection after a session or leaving the telephone and taking a break, all three of these options being available in the team situation as well, of course. It is perhaps more difficult to ensure that one does take care of oneself and use methods of support after sessions when one is working in isolation, but that is exactly why it is so essential.

An example of the way a national charity uses the telephone as part of its counselling service can be seen from the following case study.

Case Study B
CRUSE – Bereavement Care

The organisation CRUSE has been in existence for over 35 years. It provides bereavement counselling and support in a variety of ways. Over 190 local branches provide access to face to face counselling and social support groups or, for an annual membership fee subscribers to the National Membership scheme receive 10 newsletters and have the option to enter into counselling by letter with a named counsellor. CRUSE produces and sells a wide range of publications which cover aspects of bereavement and grief for adults, children and professionals as well as others which address practical matters such as funeral plans or state benefits.

The organisation also operates a telephone counselling service from its headquarters in Richmond, Surrey. The CRUSE Bereavement Counselling Line opened in 1992 and it is advertised to both CRUSE members and the public. The development of its practice to that in operation during 1995 is summarised here. Two lines are operated between 9.30 a.m. and 5 p.m., Monday–Friday. An answerphone is used out of hours to state when the service is open, but does not pick up callers' messages. If any counselling calls are received by the CRUSE switchboard, they are transferred to the Counselling Line.

There is a team of three experienced counsellors and a counselling co-ordinator who have worked within a variety of counselling orientations, but it is required that all counsellors operate within a person-centred framework. All are either qualified counsellors or trainee counsellors with at least two years' training behind them. There is also a specialist child counsellor. All are employed and paid by CRUSE and they work alongside a team of up to 10 unpaid, probationary counsellors. In addition, practical information is supplied to callers by a skilled Bereavement Welfare Rights Advisor.

CONTRACTS
The maximum length of any call is usually 60 minutes. Generally, a caller will talk with a counsellor for a single session when contact is first made. At the end of the call, the counsellor may suggest a local support group for face to face work, which may be available through a CRUSE branch or through another bereavement organisation. If there is no local group the counsellor may offer a further session by telephone; it is not always possible to guarantee that the caller will be able to speak to the same counsellor, and callers are warned of this.

The caller pays for the cost of the call, but if the caller indicates that they cannot afford it or may be calling from a call box without sufficient money, the counsellor can offer to call back.

If the counsellor believes that a more in-depth telephone counselling contract might be appropriate, they may enter into a contract with the caller of up to six one-hour weekly sessions. After that, the client will be offered ongoing letter support, for which the client is required to become a member of CRUSE. (See Chapter 8 for more about counselling by letter.)

TRAINING, SUPPORT AND SUPERVISION
Paid counsellors are recruited through a formal selection process and receive training on the job. Generally counsellors debrief each other and are expected to attend a monthly meeting with the co-ordinator, for information exchange and general discussions about issues raised during the work. There is also a monthly supervision group, facilitated by an external supervisor, of 1.5 hours' duration, attendance at which is compulsory.

Probationary counsellors all have some knowledge of basic counselling skills and receive training before joining the line. The training course covers eight modules ranging from bereavement issues to counselling by telephone: in such areas as contracts; diagnosis; telephone bereavement counselling; difficulties and distress. Once the training course has been completed, the probationary counsellors work under the direction of a paid counsellor. Their probationary period lasts for 300 hours or until the counsellor is assessed as having attained the required competency. Probationary counsellors receive formal debriefing and have regular supervision.

CASE NOTES
After each call, the counsellor is required to complete a call form as shown below. These forms are filed away and may be referred to if a caller rings back or if a counsellor wishes to raise any issue arising from the call in one of the meetings or supervision sessions.

Sample of call record sheet
CALL FORM:
CRUSE
CALLER: DATE:
ADDRESS:

Country of origin or ethnic group if known:
FOR SELF: (approximate age)
ON BEHALF OF: (approximate age/s)
CHILDREN:
. . . .
LOSS SUFFERED: LENGTH OF LOSS:
HOW DID DEATH HAPPEN:
. . . .
NATURE OF ENQUIRY AND PRESENTING PROBLEMS:

. . . .
ACTION:
LITERATURE:
Any relevant comments on service:
Length of call: Call taken by:

Susan Wallbank, the current counselling co-ordinator, believes that the telephone is an excellent medium, because of the sheer quantity of counselling which can be covered in a relatively short time; from the moment the phone is answered, the counsellor and client are straight into the session. This, and the way the service operates, supports Susan's belief that, at present, the CRUSE Bereavement Line is more closely aligned with brief therapy and crisis intervention than with long term telephone work.

Research and counselling

Gradually interest has been growing in the UK in the need to conduct research seeking evidence for the success or otherwise of aspects of counselling. Sanders and Liptrot (1993) provide some clear information about research methods for counsellors, including hints for designing and using questionnaires, and McLeod (1994a) also discusses research, in terms of different qualitative and quantitative methods.

Research into telephone counselling

How can we be sure that telephone counselling training is effective? Little research has ever been conducted formally in the UK, although increasing numbers of counselling students are considering aspects of telephone counselling as part of their degree courses. The USA, Canada and Australia have been far more inclined to support research into the use of the telephone, and the value of training and supporting workers was demonstrated by an American study.

The need for good training, support and supervision may be seen in a study reported in a paper in August 1990 by McCarthy and Reese. This paper acknowledged that while the importance of volunteers to many telephone helpline or counselling line services is clear, there seems to be a high turnover rate, with many volunteers leaving within a year or so. The study examined a number of variables related to volunteers' perceptions of stress at a particular crisis intervention agency, in an attempt to see if there were identifiable reasons which could perhaps be addressed in terms of support and supervision to prevent or to reduce the likelihood of burnout, causing people to leave the service.

The 39 volunteers in the study were aged between 22 and 50 years and had between one and 72 months' experience of working for the agency, with between 16 and 4,600 counselling hours behind them. There were 18 women and 21 men in the sample; one person was black and the rest were white.

The volunteers were given a checklist of 35 problems and were asked to rate how they would react to each of them, scoring on a 7-point Likert scale where 1 means the person rates themselves as slightly stressed and 7 as very stressed. The types of problems included working with callers who were perpetrators of domestic violence, callers who were depressed, obscene callers, callers with relationship difficulties, callers who harmed themselves or were in other life-threatening situations.

In addition there was a 12-item checklist of reasons for the stress, such as lack of knowledge, lack of skills, the problem touching on a personal issue for the counsellor, the problem being too complex, and so on. The counsellors also had to relate their reasons for and ways of dealing with the problems to their ability in using counselling skills such as open questions, reflection and allowing silences as a means of rating their own efficacy.

Not surprisingly, the volunteers experienced the different problems differently and therefore the same problem might have had all seven Likert scale ratings across the group as a whole. In general, life-threatening problems were consistently the most stressful.

Again, not surprisingly, the counsellors varied in their efficacy in dealing with the problems, and felt least effective when handling obscene calls, for example, compared with more issue-specific calls. Overall the men in the study reported a higher level of efficacy across all the problems. The most commonly endorsed reasons for stress in the group were lack of knowledge and skills and problem complexity, which suggests that ongoing training and support and supervision are all necessary to ensure the consistent delivery of a highly effective service.

Ongoing training can address knowledge-based issues and can enhance skills, while support and supervision ensure that the volunteers' general well-being is taken into account. Caring for volunteers enables them to feel valued, respected and emotionally capable of continuing to deliver high quality, effective counselling work.

Quality control in practice

It is all very well to have training, support, clear contracts, guidelines or operating procedures, but actually working to these on a
day to day basis can be another matter. It is essential that any
individual telephone counsellor or helpline worker, any supervisor or manager ensures that the practice is keeping clearly
within agreed boundaries and that work is always carried out
professionally. This requires regular consideration of the service
provided by an individual.

How does a counsellor determine whether or not her or his
work is really effective from the client's perspective? Further, how
does a counsellor maintain consistently high standards for all
clients? Supervision might be one way of addressing the latter, but
only by asking the caller can the former be really determined. Yet
if the counsellor asks the client, there will be bias in the answer.
Besides, when should the counsellor ask the client – during a
session or after all the sessions have ended? If the counsellor
works for an organisation, should it be the responsibility of the
organisation to carry out checks for quality control?

Whether face to face or on the telephone, all work should be
subject to scrutiny and not only when a complaint is made or a
counsellor asks for help. Evaluation of the service a counsellor
provides and regular monitoring of practice will aid quality
control.

Evaluation and monitoring
Some of this is addressed in the NVQ standards, in outline, but the
fine detail of what this means warrants separate, additional
consideration here.

Firstly, what is the difference between these two often used
terms? There are wide-ranging views about this, but for this book
the definition is that monitoring is an ongoing process which
includes, for example, case notes or record keeping, supervision
and supervision notes, whereas evaluation is a more thorough in-
depth review of all aspects of the service provided. For a telephone helpline this should be carried out perhaps once a year but
more likely once every two years, either by the organisation
providing the service or by an external researcher/evaluator. In a
similar way an individual counsellor could choose to have her/his
service evaluated.

In a text published in French, Jaffrin (1992) reports on an evaluation of the service 'Inter Service Parents' which was carried out as long ago as 1975 but unfortunately was never published. McLeod (1994b) refers to evaluation, or rather the lack of data about telephone counselling *processes and outcomes*. Yet there have been some detailed evaluations carried out to determine helpline counselling *efficacy*.

There is much discussion of when and how to evaluate a telephone helpline service. Among the methods used, that of talking to the service users is one of the most difficult to arrange and yet is perhaps the one method most likely to give a true and accurate view of how the service is experienced. Another commonly used method is to send questionnaires to some service users. These have a notoriously low return rate (averaging about 30 per cent) and tend to consist of praising rather than appraising the service received – in other words those who found the service helpful are most likely to return the forms. While one can then speculate about the other 70 per cent, true, hard data of the efficacy of a service are hard to come by. Indeed, the service efficacy is often determined through anecdotal feedback or by monitoring an organisation's formal complaints procedure.

Helpline Evaluation – Guidelines for Helplines Seeking to Conduct an Evaluation of their Service (Telephone Helplines Association, 1995a) takes the perspective that evaluation of a service is essential. This is not only for personal (and personnel) development and to ensure that the service is of the highest possible quality and meets stated objectives, but also to satisfy those providing funds for the service that the money is used as anticipated and, most important of all, that the service is beneficial to users. Evaluation has been seen as an integral part of a few services for some time, but it is gradually becoming a prerequisite for funding to be given.

It is hard to provide a confidential service and then to ask questions of the callers after the initial helpline call, but organisations which have endeavoured to do this often use an external researcher who talks to the caller, asking specific questions. Clearly there must be a measure of flexibility in who is passed on to the researcher or evaluator – a very distressed caller is not likely to be asked to participate, and indeed anyone asked must have the option to refuse. Those who do participate are likely to be passed on to speak to the evaluator there and then. In a few studies, the evaluators have asked permission of those questioned to call them again some weeks later. This is to ascertain whether or not the impact of the helpline call was long lasting and how much of what had been discussed in the call had been useful to the caller over a period of time. In some cases when the caller was re-contacted they did not wish to be re-interviewed, but data, however small they are sometimes in quantity, are being gathered gradually across a number of different services.

Evaluation of the effectiveness of a telephone service
One American attempt to evaluate the effectiveness of an anonymous telephone helpline service was reported in a survey by Gingerich et al. (1988). The service providers were interested in determining the impact the service had on a caller's situation and carried out its evaluation by interviewing callers. Counsellors were asked to invite callers to participate in research about the service and if they agreed the callers were asked if they would be willing to receive a follow-up call from a researcher within two weeks of the original call.

Immediately it can be seen that the evaluation cannot be totally objective. The subjectivity involved in which callers were selected by the counsellors to be asked to participate is the reason for this. In addition, not all the counsellors were willing to join the study. Those counsellors who did take part spoke to about 400 callers during the period. Between 25 per cent and 30 per cent of these callers were not asked to participate. A similar percentage were asked but declined to take part and 10–15 per cent of those who did agree could not be contacted at the time of the follow-up interview. This meant that out of a possible 8,000 callers to the whole service during the period of the research, and 400 who might have taken part, only 171 people participated in the study.

Nevertheless, the study highlights that for 90 per cent of these callers, the session with the counsellor was rated as helpful and the clients all said that they would want to call again if the need arose. More than half the clients reported that their problem had improved after the call while just over a third reported no change and almost 10 per cent rated the problem as worse.

As the researchers report, account must be taken of the fact that it is possible some problems would have seemed less severe to the individual whether or not the person had spoken with the counsellor in the first place, simply because time and circumstances move on. A point to take into consideration with the clients who said their problem had got worse is that the clients might have contacted other sources of help, which might have had some bearing on the problem and its lack of resolution.

It is clear that there are imperfections in this study, but it is important because it tried to do something which many counsellors and counselling organisations seem to be reluctant to attempt: it asked the users for their views using independent researchers who did not have a personal interest in the outcome.

Evaluation of individual one to one counselling

What has all of this evaluation and monitoring got to do with telephone counselling? Apart from when a client makes a formal complaint about a counsellor to the British Association for Counselling for example, there is little way of assessing how a client fares after counselling, unless the client chooses to re-contact or to seek help elsewhere, when the original counsellor might be informed or the new source might be told by the client of previous experiences of seeking help.

It seems to me that it could be very useful to ask clients who finish their sessions whether it would be possible for someone to contact them in three months' time to ask them how they are faring as part of an overall piece of research not focused solely on that one person. In this way, it might be feasible to assess the impact of the counselling on a number of clients. The person contacting could be the counsellor's supervisor or a researcher, although it is acknowledged that it might be too expensive to employ a researcher for the evaluation of only a small number of clients.

The exercise would be an independent way of monitoring the counsellor as well as assessing the impact of the counselling. It would not be useful for the counsellor to make the calls, since this could put pressure on the client to seek to appease or to please the counsellor. Whilst elsewhere in this book it is stated that the telephone provides a safer medium than being in the same room as the counsellor for the client to express emotion, it is likely to be hard, nevertheless, for the client to give negative feedback to the counsellor. Further, it could compromise the counsellor–client relationship which had previously existed by forcing it to develop in quite a different dimension.

Asking the same questions of each client should provide a measure of both the counsellor's and the counselling process's effectiveness in terms of desired outcome as expressed by the client.

There are, of course, issues associated with confidentiality to consider here. Offering the client the option of using a pseudonym, ensuring that the questions are broad and open ended and reassuring the client of the purpose of the research and that they will not be personally identifiable to the researcher, ensures that most clients are likely to agree to participate. If the counsellor calls the client and then hands the telephone over to the researcher or writes to the client beforehand, asking the client to call the researcher directly, the client's telephone number need not be known to the researcher, further enhancing confidentiality.

This evaluation of the counselling process, its impact on the client and evaluation of the counsellor's performance need not be exclusive to telephone counselling clients; why not introduce it for use with face to face clients too?

4

Theoretical Orientations

In observing and listening to trained counsellors and to others with no formal counselling training working on a variety of telephone helplines, it is to be noted that there is often intense (self-imposed) pressure to come up with a solution to the problem(s) heard, at the expense of working only with what the caller wishes to bring, particularly among those new to telephone work. This 'need to solve' may be quite different to the style of the counsellor's professional face to face counselling orientation.

It seems that the nature of telephone counselling can evoke, even may require, a more proactive stance on the part of a counsellor, whether or not the caller has the option to contact the same counsellor again. This makes certain theoretical orientations less likely to be adapted successfully to the telephone than others. McLeod (1993) highlights the lack of clear theory or research into telephone counselling and gives some consideration to the question of modifying techniques and to the types of issues or problems which might be appropriate for telephone work. Overall, those orientations which follow humanistic or cognitive-behavioural theory – where a person is encouraged to become conscious of, and to control, many aspects of behaviour – seem to be more adaptable to the telephone than are psychoanalytic orientations, where a person is said to be influenced by instincts set in childhood and counselling seeks ultimately to strengthen the 'ego' by reducing childhood repressions.

Transference and countertransference

Earlier in this book it was stated that telephone counselling usually contains an element of transference and countertransference. Here we will explore this a little more before moving on to consider specific counselling and therapeutic styles.

Transference and countertransference may be thought of in terms of 'informing your intuition'. Traditionally, transference and countertransference can be defined as projections, commonly used to describe the unconscious, emotional bonds that arise between two persons in an analytic or therapeutic relationship (Jacoby, 1984). Consider transference and countertransference broadly as interactions which exist to some degree in every relationship, whether or not they are perceived or acted upon. If this is so, it could be argued that in any instance of telephone counselling the existence and use of empathy in the relationship is in fact comparable with transference/countertransference. This is because empathy is part of the interaction of the client and the counsellor which exists only in that way between those two people and it would not be exactly the same were that client talking with a different counsellor.

From another perspective, if the counsellor is carrying out telephone counselling for an organisation rather than as a private individual, then there must be some awareness of the possibility that the client will perceive either the counsellor or the organisation as a 'good person' and the other as a 'bad person'. This splitting must be addressed by the counsellor in working with the client once it is recognised to exist, in order to ensure that the therapeutic relationship between the client and counsellor can continue to develop in a 'healthy' way.

With some psychotherapeutic orientations it is essential that the interpretation, development and working through of transference takes place as a fundamental part of the therapy. A counsellor must be very clear whether this is desirable and can be worked with constructively as part of the counselling process, or whether what is happening is unhelpfully connected to assumptions and projections and has to be addressed or challenged in a different way.

The need to be aware of this difference comes because it is all too easy, when the phone is the only contact between client and counsellor, for the client to relate to the counsellor like someone else from their past/current experience. Similarly, it is all too easy for the counsellor to get drawn into this and into any story the client is relating with regard to this person, whether this is based in fact or not.

The counsellor has to decide how to address this, which can be quite challenging. Pointing out what is happening too soon for the client could lead to the client feeling undermined or patronised. This could encourage the client to end the sessions there and then. Leaving it too long could evoke denial from the client and resistance to continuing to explore issues or feelings. Words like 'might' rather than 'should' and phrases like 'it seems that what you have told me about your sister's behaviour towards you and what you think I might be feeling . . .' rather than 'You [the client] are confusing me with your sister' are less likely to patronise or evoke denial. Allowing the client to tell the counsellor that the counsellor is wrong, rather than that the client is at fault, can help to address projections and prevent trans-ference material from getting in the way of or dominating the relationship.

Cognitive-behavioural therapies

The telephone as a counselling medium can fit well with cognitive-behavioural therapeutic approaches. The emphasis in these is for the client to have focused tasks or goals which are then developed in their thinking processes in sessions. These therapies can work well by telephone because they require the client to be an active participant, empowered by the process of the work and the counsellor–client *partnership*.

Dryden and Feltham (1992) point out that it is well established that counselling works better from the client's point of view when the client feels involved and consulted. If the client is encouraged to participate in the process of counselling from the outset, not only does the client understand what counselling might be about, but she or he also becomes aware of how the process might be useful to them. In the same book, Dryden and Feltham talk of brief counselling as any counselling that lasts from one to 20 sessions or so, where the sessions may be consecutive and weekly or spread further apart. These two aspects of partnership and contract fit well with many telephone services either where counselling is offered or, as in the case of the majority of helplines, where counselling skills are used extensively in the relationship with the caller. The intention often is to assist the caller to seek their own answers to the specific problem they present or to aid the caller to make decisions about a specific issue. One example of a range of situations for which telephone cognitive-behavioural therapy is particularly useful is in working with people who have phobias or for those who suffer from panic attacks.

Cognitive-analytic therapy

Cognitive-analytic therapy (CAT) (Ryle, 1990) is another model of therapy requiring active participation by both the client and the therapist. The emphasis on the use and exchange of written material between counsellor and client might make this particular therapy harder, although not impossible, to carry out by telephone compared with face to face as it would also require and rely on good postal or fax communication.

Originally based on rational emotive therapy, CAT is quite analytic in style and it integrates aspects of psychoanalysis, Kelly's Personal Construct Theory, cognitive-behavioural approaches and developmental and cognitive psychology (see also McCormick, 1996). Compared with other types of analytic therapy, CAT is quite brief, with 16 sessions generally being offered as an initial contract and a follow-up session approximately three months after this, which may lead to further sessions.

Person-centred counselling

Client or person-centred counselling lends itself well to telephone work. Carl Rogers (1987: 30) stated that 'client-centred counselling, if it is to be effective, cannot be a trick or a tool. It is not a subtle way of guiding the client while pretending to let him guide himself. To be effective, it must be genuine.' As a guiding principle, this attitude to the client, which highlights respect within the relationship, underlines what must take place on the phone: a counsellor must attend to the client totally and convey this to the client.

Mearns and Thorne (1989) quote Bozarth and Temaner Brodley (1986) and detail a 'Person Centred Counsellor's Creed' or set of beliefs, which include the following:

– that every individual has internal resources for growth;
– that human nature is essentially constructive and social;
– that self-regard is a basic human need;
– that persons are motivated to seek the truth;
– that perceptions determine experience and behaviour;
– that the individual should be the primary reference point in any helping activity.

All of these can be explored using the telephone as a medium for counselling. Indeed many helplines (knowingly or otherwise) operate along person-centred lines, whether the service is one of the minority offering counselling or one of the majority offering counselling skills.

Process-oriented psychology

Process-oriented psychology (POP) is an approach which has roots in Jungian psychology, Taoism and physics and was developed in 1969 by a Jungian analyst and physicist, Dr Arnold Mindell. Mindell came to believe that body experiences and symptoms mirror dreams and are expressions of the unconscious mind. The process that expresses itself through both the dream and the body is termed the 'dreambody'. With a focus on exploring the meaning behind a problem rather than working with a cause, POP seeks to enable clients to find solutions through raised awareness of what is happening and what they are experiencing, this being its method and only goal. It avoids interpretation and specific programmes.

Since the work with a client is varied according to the client's changing needs, POP can include elements of psychotherapy, such as work with dreams, or might involve art or drama therapy or even a conversation with a client. It can be carried out with people in altered or extreme states such as in a coma or with a psychiatric illness.

Therapy may be with the individual, families or groups, and can be used in organisational development and conflict resolution. As many current trainees are involved in working by telephone to

some degree and/or use the phone for some training or supervision, this approach is explained in more detail than others in this
chapter.

Training

Training takes at least five years, involves taking examinations and
is individually created for each student working with a group or
study committee of at least three members, two of whom must be
studying for or qualified POP diplomates. There are around 40
students throughout the UK and lectures and seminars are held by
visiting POP diplomates from as far afield as Zurich and Oregon.
The first UK diplomates have just finished their training. It is
hoped that this will make process work more accessible in the UK.

At present some students, such as Charlotte Willoughby, have
their own therapy by telephone with diplomates based in other
countries. Charlotte has sessions every three weeks or so with a
therapist based in Poland. The sessions last for an hour and
Charlotte calls her therapist each time. She pays for the sessions
by international money order after a few sessions rather than after
each one. The work with her therapist involves being aware of
her physical as well as her emotional experience during the
session. She might, for example, notice herself making a gesture
and will bring that into the session. Process work involves the
verbal, the visual, feelings, movements and the relationship with
the therapist as sources of information.

Charlotte, who also has some of her supervision by phone,
enjoys working by phone, liking the fact that she has to be really
clear and specific in order to convey all her thoughts and gestures
and to develop an explicit awareness of the non-visual actions she
makes.

Psychodynamic orientations

A psychodynamic orientation, such as Freudian, post-Freudian or
Jungian analysis and the psychodynamic counselling approaches
developed from these, may be considered in a generalised way to
be fundamentally based on the interpretation and working
through of the patient's thoughts, dreams and feelings around an
experience in order to undo and resolve unsatisfactory defences
and conflicts. Paramount in this process is the relationship and the
dependency between the client and the therapist.

Clearly there is no couch on the telephone and entering and leaving the room does not occur as it does in psychodynamic therapy, when interpretation may be made of any attempt by the patient to engage the therapist in conversation before or after the formal start or ending of the session. In the case of telephone work, the phone rings, is answered and requires at least a greeting 'hello' to ensure the correct number has been dialled and the correct person has answered the phone. Further, in the classical psychoanalytic tradition the therapist is silent except when making an interpretation, which is not likely to be very successful on the telephone, when clients often require encouragement and verbal gestures, such as 'mmms' as described earlier in Chapter 2, to be clear that the counsellor or therapist is still there and listening and conveying interest.

It follows that the interaction required on the telephone and the lack of visual clues and cues would make it unlikely at first glance that a counsellor with strong psychoanalytic methods of working or a psychotherapist of these schools would find the telephone a suitable medium. On the other hand, it could be argued that the telephone could enhance transference and for that reason might be a very useful medium.

Alvin Mahrer's work in experiential psychotherapy (1989) is in some respects a bit of a halfway house between traditional psychoanalytic therapy and telephone counselling, having features which are associated with using the telephone for therapy. Mahrer and his client both lie on reclining chairs placed parallel to each other and both he and the client close their eyes. By so doing, he believes, there is better access to the client's inner world and a reduction in unnecessary 'role relationships'.

While one could extend the examples above to other orientations and theories, it is perhaps becoming clearer that telephone counselling and telephone psychotherapy have aspects of practice which do not fit neatly into any single orientation used for face to face work. It seems as if the telephone is a good medium for many of the models of brief counselling, but in summary it might be more accurate to state that both telephone counselling and psychotherapy are a conglomeration of theories and practices and defy simple labelling. Indeed, for counsellors, its flexibility of approach is one of the medium's greatest assets. The telephone brings the opportunity to have the experience of counselling to a wide audience, as will be seen in the next chapter.

Case Study C
Psychotherapy by telephone

Some traditionally trained psychotherapists are using the telephone in their work. One such therapist is Wolf who has a traditional psychotherapeutic background; having undergone Freudian analysis and trained as a Freudian psychotherapist, he later followed this with a Winnicottian analysis. Wolf has also worked as a social worker; in training for this profession he was taught by Winnicott.

While Wolf does not believe that the telephone can be a complete substitute for traditional analysis with patient and therapist in the same room, he does use the telephone in certain circumstances in a complementary fashion or when the traditional model can no longer be used for specific reasons such as chronic illness or the patient moving away.

By way of example, Wolf has a patient with whom he works on the telephone. The patient had worked with him for more than five years in the traditional setting before moving to another part of the UK. The fact that the ongoing therapeutic alliance had already been established is a critical factor. Wolf does not think that psychotherapy could best be conducted by telephone unless there has been a prior, traditional relationship.

This patient calls Wolf at a fixed appointment time each week, for a 50-minute session. Payment is made by cheque once a month and any change in fees is negotiated on the phone. Although initially Wolf himself thought the sessions would be short term, perhaps while the patient sought a new, local therapist, they have in fact continued working together on the phone for more than a year at the time of writing.

One might argue that the patient is unable to find a new therapist while still maintaining the previous relationship, but Wolf is clear that part of his responsibility as a therapist is to work with the patient so that the patient can leave when ready to do so. Wolf believes that it is important that any patient knows that he will be there as long as the patient needs him and that patients do reach a point at which they no longer need the psychotherapist. When a final session is agreed with this patient, it will take place with the patient coming back to see Wolf, as he believes it is important to end as they had begun, in the traditional manner.

Another patient who is seeing Wolf regularly, and has been working with him for many years, has chronic poor health and if the patient is not well enough to attend for a session, the patient will phone instead and therapist and patient will have their 50 minutes by telephone.

The key to his work is flexibility and Wolf has found that there are differences between the nature of the actual telephone sessions he has and those he conducts with a patient who visits and with whom he has eye to eye contact. He has found, for example, that telephone sessions seem to be more free for himself – he is not giving anything away as the therapist if he moves his hands while talking on the telephone.

Wolf also experiences some practical similarities and differences with his work in the two settings:

- The patient who is lying down on the couch does not have any eye contact with the therapist, just as there would be no eye contact by telephone.
- When engaged in a telephone session, Wolf has found that neither party is distracted by extraneous matters, which is similar to his experience of working with patients who use the couch compared with sitting in a chair.
- Projection mechanisms operate similarly face to face and on the telephone, and how any therapist works with transference and how much it is made explicit depends on the therapist's practice and not on the medium.
- The most obvious difference is that which has already been highlighted for counsellors: the lack of visual clues as to the patient's state – perhaps in the physical appearance or style of dress in that session compared to previous sessions – and certainly the lack of visual body language to accompany the words (or silences) makes the telephone sessions quite dissimilar to sessions conducted in the same room.
- The entering and leaving the room is a part of the session which is clearly omitted on the telephone and is not replaced by anything as specific.

Wolf is a supervisor who gives face to face supervision. In exceptional circumstances these are supplemented by telephone sessions with his supervisees.

As a psychotherapist, Wolf believes that 'the interpretations [he] makes are of [his] understanding and capacity to conceptualise and verbalise the thoughts and feelings expressed by the patient in a meaningful way to the patient'. As such they may take place on the telephone, with the qualifications described above, or in the same room as the patient.

Sandra L. Fish (1987) acknowledges that the use of the telephone for short term (possibly anonymous) crisis counselling is accepted and she quotes traditional therapy as being 'contact between the therapist and client leading to change in the client's behaviors which interfere with work or social relationships, bringing substantial change in perspective'.

She then explains that she thinks that traditional therapy is in the process of being redefined, expanded and decentralised by the telephone and by other forms of mediated communication such as the radio phone-in, on television and by computer (see also Chapter 8). While this is not a bad thing, she suggests, it raises the very important issue of the need to bring the redefinition into line with good, ethical practice: 'just as copyright laws designed to protect the authors of print are inapplicable to video and are [therefore] being revised, so the rules of traditional therapy are undergoing re-definition [to meet the requirements of the new media]'.

It is essential that the professional bodies representing the worlds of counselling and psychotherapy in the UK, too, acknowledge the need to adapt and redefine some of their work and ethical codes and practices to ensure that the telephone client is protected and has the right to high standards of service, as does any face to face client.

5

The Counsellor–Client Relationship

Telephone counselling stretches the skills and the mind. It can be both challenging and exciting for a counsellor to work in this medium. Although theoretically there is no limit to the number of clients a counsellor could work with each day, four clients is suggested as a maximum daily total. For many telephone counsellors this will mean four hours of client contact divided equally between four clients (see below: 'Negotiating a contract'). This enables adequate writing up/debriefing after each client and ensures that the counsellor remains alert and responsive to each client as a separate individual. Bearing in mind the intensity of working by telephone, 'time out' is essential for telephone counsellors, no matter how experienced they might be.

Telephone counselling is appropriate for a wide range of clients; anyone, in fact, who is comfortable with the telephone and has access to a telephone with privacy. It must not be forgotten that anyone using the phone for counselling must be able to do so from a place in which they feel physically safe. People who suffer from agoraphobia and are unable to go out can take obvious advantage of telephone counselling. People who are physically disabled can enter counselling using the telephone with far greater practical ease than they might otherwise find. Similarly, people who live in rural areas or are in isolated locations, shift workers or those who seek to work with a specific counsellor who might not practise in their locality may all prefer to work on the telephone.

Clearly, there may be a financial issue to consider here. How much would the call to the counsellor cost per session, in addition to any fee? This may be a situation for negotiation at the time of agreeing a counselling contract (see below). For any potential client, an additional key motive may be that of saving time – the time that would be taken up with travelling to get to the counsellor's practice. It might be an easier and more attractive proposition to fit in a regular session by telephone and to plan around it with no concerns about the reliability of public or private transport. By having to allocate only the time allotted for the session and perhaps a few minutes afterwards for reflection, telephone counselling can be perceived as less intrusive to a client's world in a practical sense. For some clients this can make the whole concept of counselling far less threatening or intimidating and more acceptable.

Working by phone can be very liberating for the counsellor. No need to tidy up the counselling room or even to have a separate room, as long as the place where the counsellor sits during the session is free from external distractions. There is no need to be concerned about the clothes one puts on, whether or not one 'looks the part', has clean hair or any other physical, personal detail!

If working from an office base in a room with other people around, it is essential that the counsellor can convey and give total attention to the client. This requires the co-operation of colleagues who must be aware that they should not approach the desk or interrupt when a counsellor is on the phone. The counsellor might find that using a headset rather than a handset on the telephone helps to cut out background distractions. An additional benefit derived from using a good quality headset is that it helps to prevent the client from picking up background noise from the counsellor's surroundings (see also Chapter 7). It might also be possible to have some degree of soundproofing around the counsellor's area by dividing it off from the other parts of the office with screens.

How does a client choose a telephone counsellor?

Here, I am not referring to the contact a person has when they ring a helpline or telephone befriending service and speak to whoever happens to be on duty at the time. Rather, I am referring to formally arranged counselling.

In a face to face situation, a client may call or visit one or several counsellors who have been personally recommended or who are listed on a local or national resource list. If the initial contact is by phone, the client will often be offered a first visit before sessions formally begin to meet with the counsellor at the appointed venue. Both parties may then reserve the right to choose not to go further with the relationship and this trial session may be free of charge.

If a client is seeking telephone counselling, they may wish to call different counsellors and talk informally with them, since a visit is not going to be appropriate, but what will help the client to choose? On a fundamental level, the telephone client has to feel comfortable with the counsellor's tone of voice, accent, vocabulary and general manner if the relationship is to be established and if the client is to trust in the counsellor. These are not easily measurable or describable factors, but are more a case of 'gut instinct' or 'chemistry' between two people.

It is to be hoped that national organisations such as the British Association for Counselling will soon formally recognise telephone counselling as an entity in its own right, particularly as the NVQs now exist (see Chapter 3) and might enable counsellors who offer this to be listed separately. This will provide a means for potential clients to choose a counsellor. Some helplines offer referral services and might be willing to add telephone counsellors to their lists. At the time of writing this book, there is no formal telephone counselling referral network, so clients are heavily reliant on personal contact and recommendation between organisations or individual counsellors.

Telephone counselling and boundaries

Apart from an overall boundary of the total number of clients with whom a counsellor should work in a day, boundaries need to be established which cover a wide range of issues. These should be addressed in a preliminary session which is arranged at the time of the initial telephone contact and which is explicitly not the first counselling session. Some people will wish to use the space to 'off-load' and the counsellor must be clear about how much of that can be done and what should be curtailed for a further session. The preliminary session should take place without becoming a counselling session no matter how insistent the potential client seems, just as a face to face counsellor should not probe by phone or allow the potential client to 'off-load' when the person makes first contact. Incidentally, this highlights a difference between telephone counselling and helpline work, where this initial contact might be the only contact.

In simply speaking to the counsellor on the phone to arrange an appointment time for the preliminary session, the client will begin to think about the person they have contacted. How did the voice sound? What sort of impression did the counsellor create? If the image is favourable and comfortable, the client may be more confident during the preliminary session. It is important to remember, of course, that the client may be concerned about the image she or he believes might have been conveyed to the counsellor, which could make for an uneasy start to the preliminary session.

The preliminary session

Negotiating a contract
As with all counselling, the negotiation of the contract is very important. For telephone counselling the contract should address at least all of the following:

How frequently will sessions be held?   Once-weekly sessions is a good starting point and will be appropriate for most telephone counselling but there might be times when fortnightly is more suitable, perhaps as part of an ending process. The counsellor must be clear about whether or not the client can have more frequent sessions such as for short, crisis periods, but should be aware that it can be very easy to encourage too great a dependency by being so readily accessible – a client is far more likely to pick up the phone than make an unscheduled visit to the counsellor.

How long will each session last?   The traditional therapeutic hour of 50 minutes works well by telephone. This then enables 10 minutes for recovery and debriefing and is in total a 'tidy', manageable package of time. It often seems as if the first 15 minutes of a session go quite slowly, particularly with new clients, and then the remaining 35 fly by. This is perhaps because it takes some time for both client and counsellor to relax into the session and to differentiate it as not being the same as a telephone conversation with a friend. Any session longer than 60 minutes, especially when the sessions are weekly, is less likely to be productive in encouraging clients to work for themselves between sessions. Quite apart from that, literally holding a receiver, focusing and concentrating so intensely for more than 60 minutes can be tiring and the 'recovery time' post-session needs to be increased from whatever the counsellor finds adequate in a session of 60 minutes or less. Unless one party is unwell or cannot concentrate for up to an hour, sessions shorter than 45 or 50 minutes are less likely to be helpful if a true counselling process is to take place. If, for example, a client wishes to end a session after 20 minutes, it may be because that is the point at which the session is becoming uncomfortable or too intense. Although the counsellor cannot actually stop the client from hanging up, a clear contract will provide the counsellor with a starting point to address and explore the client's wish to end the session rather than continuing for the full time period as agreed.

How many sessions will there be before a review? Again this should be agreed at the outset. At least six weekly, hour-long sessions would be a good place to start, since this gives time for both parties to begin to get to know each other's voice tones and patterns, get a sense of each other and start to explore issues therapeutically rather than in an anecdotal fashion. It can be easy to slip into being told about a situation without stopping and asking the client to explore surrounding issues and feelings and perhaps even challenging the client. By the time there has been six sessions, enough trust should have been built up for the counsellor to have been able to establish a relationship with the client. A review can give the client the opportunity to feed back how this has felt and will give the counsellor some idea of the pace which might be needed for future sessions to feel safe enough and be productive. There should be regular reviews, perhaps every four to six weeks, which might take most or, more usually, part of a session. Setting these up clearly in advance after the first review can help a client to keep attending. Knowing that one has a review due can be like setting a goal; reaching the next review can make the client feel that something has been achieved in terms of commitment. The telephone as a medium makes it easier for a client not to attend than is the case in face to face sessions (see below), so agreed review targets can be very useful 'milestones'.

What sort of privacy will there be for both parties during the session? The whole question of background noise and the need for both parties to be able to concentrate has already been considered, but part of the contract negotiation has to include some discussion about where the client will be for the sessions, the likelihood of interruptions and how these will be managed.

The client must be able to ensure that for telephone counselling sessions she or he is alone in a quiet room separate from other distractions in order to be able to attend fully to the sessions. The client may need to arrange to have a physical space and period of time when no one else is around. This could involve complex arrangements for child care for example, and the degree of commitment this may necessitate for the client should be talked through before the first session starts.

How will the client pay, if at all? Will payment be in advance or after a session? What will happen if the cheque or postal order does not arrive in time? Should the counsellor provide some self-addressed envelopes for clients to use for sending payment? There are many questions connected with payment for the session, but part of the contract should include clear discussion and agreement of the fees and how and when the client will pay. It might be feasible to ask the client to pay in advance for a month or for the number of sessions between reviews, or to ask for weekly payment post-session. Assuming that the client calls the counsellor, there is no need to include the cost of the counsellor's phone call in the fee negotiation, but the counsellor might wish to take this cost into account when setting the fee. It might be agreed that the client will pay the day after the session by post, so that the payment should arrive before the next (weekly) session, although this might not always be the case if, for example, the client lives outside the UK.

Who will call whom? The issue of who calls whom is raised in the previous paragraph in financial terms, but it is more usual for the client to phone the counsellor at the appointed time than vice versa. This indicates the client's commitment and awareness of the relationship: it is significant enough for the client to remember when to call. If the client lives far away and the session would involve a long-distance call, this might affect the time of the day when the sessions are held. For example, if either party is overseas there may be time differences to take into account.

Does the client wish to keep the sessions completely confidential from others in their life? If so, is the client aware that if calling the counsellor from home, there could be a breach in the client's confidentiality because the call will be listed on the client's itemised phone bill? Similarly, the counsellor who calls the client might wish to ensure that their own phone number is barred from being revealed through call return (see Chapter 7). This is also linked to the question of privacy raised above and who else might be at the client's location when the sessions are held. There might be times of the day or week when the client could be totally alone and undisturbed, which could provide an optimum time for the session(s).

What could necessitate a breach of confidentiality and why? There must be clear boundaries as to when, if ever, the counsellor would contact someone else about the client, for example the client's GP. Similarly, there must be clear boundaries as to when, if ever, the counsellor would breach confidentiality: because, for example, the client disclosed that they were doing something illegal, that they were sexually abusing a child, were suicidal or were involved in fraudulent or terrorist activities (see also Bond, 1993). *It is essential to agree the broad basis of confidentiality at the outset.* If it is important for the counsellor to know next of kin, GP details or employer details for example, the counsellor should explain why, and when, if ever, such people might be contacted by the counsellor. It is, of course, unlikely that a counsellor would go into great detail about some of the specific issues listed here with a new client. On the other hand, if during a session the counsellor perceives that the client might be about to say something which could lead to the counsellor having to breach confidentiality, the counsellor must take responsibility to warn the client: 'If you carry on talking along the lines you have started, you need to know that I might need to disclose part of this session to _____ because what you might be telling me could be an illegal act.' Any telephone counsellor working with people under the age of 18 must be aware of specific child-protection situations when confidentiality may need to be broken.

What happens if the client is not available at the allotted time? How much leeway will the counsellor allow for the client to be late in calling or for how long will the counsellor try if the client's line is engaged? If the client is due to call and does not, it must have been agreed in advance by both parties what time limit there will be to the sessions commencing. If the client calls five minutes late, the counsellor might still hold the full session, or might cut it short by five minutes. If the counsellor is due to call the client, how many attempts are made to contact the client if the line is engaged?

What constitutes a no-show? If the client calls more than 10 minutes late, will the session be forfeited? How long will the counsellor wait for the client to call before deciding the session is not going to take place, and what happens if the client calls after that but still within the allotted appointment time? In general, it can be more helpful to hold the session but to ensure that it ends at what would have been the true ending time and to work with the impact of the shortened session during that session or the next. If the client does not call at all, will the counsellor attempt to make contact before the next scheduled session or not? Unless there is some clear reason why the counsellor should initiate contact, it would seem more appropriate for the counsellor to wait for the client to re-contact. If the client calls before the next session to explain and seeks a session then and there, will it take place? It is unlikely that a counsellor would offer a session on demand but see 'What happens . . . call in crisis', below. If a client does not call at the agreed time for perhaps two sessions, at that point the counsellor might *write* to the client to see whether or not they wish to continue with sessions. It can be very difficult for the client who might wish to drop out of telephone counselling to do so if the counsellor tries to make contact by phone following a couple of no-shows.

What happens if the counsellor is not available at the agreed time? Except in an emergency, when the counsellor should ensure that the client is contacted somehow, there is no excuse for the counsellor to be late or unavailable. If the contract is for both parties to talk at a specific time each week, it must be the counsellor's priority to be there.

What happens if the client chooses to call in crisis outside of the scheduled sessions? It is important from the first session that the counsellor makes explicit how late into the evening or how early in the morning or on what days of the week any client can call. Some counsellors do permit an interim 'holding' session, if the client rings and asks for one in a crisis, although it is unlikely that the client will get the session when they ring; instead they may be asked to call back at a specified time. It may not be possible to define exactly what the counsellor offers, if anything, in terms of interim sessions at the outset, as it may vary for different clients. A general principle at the start of the relationship that the sessions are held regularly with reviews offers the counsellor or client the opportunity to address the issue of frequency at a review. Of course, when a client rings up distressed two days before a session, it is very hard not to be drawn into talking with them. In such a case, the counsellor should be clear that this cannot be a full session (unless of course the counsellor thinks a full session is appropriate) but the counsellor might be available for up to 15 minutes in the capacity of doing a 'holding job', that is, exploring why the client feels the crisis is *now* and helping the client to work out what they can do for themselves until the next session. This may seem hard, but some clients find difficulty in using (structured) telephone sessions and if they are always able to get crisis management help between sessions, why should they struggle with the counselling process? Indeed, people who call helplines often do so at times of crisis with a need to talk through the immediate issue(s) and seek support, which is a good illustration of one of the key differences between the *telephone counselling skills* which most helplines offer and *telephone counselling*.

What happens if either party is ill? This is something which can be discussed at the first session when negotiating the contract, in terms of what period of notice is required for a cancellation, whether or not the client will still have to pay and whether a replacement session will be offered. It is often likely that a client will attend a telephone session when they might feel too ill to go outside and would not have struggled to a face to face session.

Similarly, if the counsellor is not feeling well, it might just be possible to hold the session nevertheless. This will obviously depend on the illness.

How will the client 'leave the room'? It is essential that the counsellor discuss the time immediately after the session with the client. Clients could be encouraged to take some time after each session to reflect on the session, perhaps to have a cup of coffee or to write down, draw or tape-record, just for themselves, anything they hold from the session, before going back to any other activity. These are all ways of 'leaving the room', as would happen physically if a client was attending a counsellor's premises, and it is important because the client does not have the travelling time to 'debrief', as they would from a face to face session.

Can either party eat or drink during a session? It is easy to pick up that someone is eating, drinking, smoking, chewing, doodling or doing anything else which can be a distraction to the session, and all of these should be discouraged. It is one thing which people who are calling from home often do not consider might be an issue – part of preparing for the session might be to put on the kettle, make a drink and settle down to talk – so it is always worth pointing out if it is not acceptable and why.

What notes, if any, will both parties take? This raises other questions, such as will any sessions be taped, what records will be kept and for how long? If any records are held on computer, they must comply with the Data Protection Registrar's requirements and taping of sessions without both parties' permission is illegal (see also Chapter 7). However, notes made as debriefing after a session can be useful for both parties and for the counsellor's supervision.

It is worth remembering that the turning of a page, the act of moving a pen across a paper will often be heard and can be interpreted as lack of interest, not paying sufficient attention to the other person or avoidance of an issue. In any case, the reason for any background noise should be explored or explained by either party to prevent this from becoming a reason for fantasy or distorted thinking. The counsellor might need to take a lead in this action, in order that the client knows that they have 'permission' to respond in kind.

If the client hangs up, what next? Although this might not be explicit at the very first session, it might need to be discussed at a review session in terms of whether either party re-contacts. Does the counsellor wait till next session? Can the client call before the next session? The answer to this might depend on the counselling orientation. It may take the form of assuming that the client will call again at the next agreed session time. If this session does not take place, the counsellor might write to suggest that they will hold two further sessions open for the client. After this, if neither session is used, the counsellor will assume that the client wishes to end the sessions. By making written contact the counsellor can state these terms clearly; it might be more difficult to try to talk to a reluctant client by telephone, since the client will either not come to the phone or could seek to use the contact as a session. One cautionary note: it is just possible that the session could be broken because of something untoward like freak weather conditions, so if the client seems to hang up, it can be helpful for the counsellor to think about the immediate seconds before this occurred. If the client was in full flow and not distressed in any way, is it likely that the session would have been deliberately terminated?

What is deemed acceptable behaviour by both the counsellor and the client? The BAC Code of Ethics states what is acceptable behaviour for a professional counsellor so that a client (or anyone else) knows what can be expected, and Bond (1993) also refers to standards of good practice, but there are other areas which might need to be clarified. If a counsellor will not tolerate racial abuse, for example, it is the counsellor's responsibility to inform the client of this and what action the counsellor will take should the client say something that the counsellor finds offensive in this context. As another example, some counsellors do not like to hear swearing and again must inform the clients of this. If a client's natural speech uses swear words as adjectives it might not be appropriate for such a counsellor to work with this client.

Most of these areas should be talked through at the preliminary session and could be confirmed in writing to the client to ensure that the counsellor has made an accurate interpretation of the discussion and to formalise the start of the relationship. Any issues not explicit at this time might need discussion at a review session, as indicated earlier.

Further issues for consideration before the sessions begin

Questions

It is important that sufficient time is provided, as well as the opportunity, for some questioning of the counsellor during the preliminary session, to take into account the lack of face to face contact and the assumptions that are made in a face to face encounter. It is quite likely that the client will want to check facts or ask questions of the counsellor, although the client might not have the courage to ask any 'personal' questions. Some face to face counselling orientations prohibit this direct questioning, or at least do not encourage giving direct answers, but being able to create an image of some aspects of the unseen counsellor can be very important and can help in establishing a telephone relationship. A strictly psychodynamic counsellor or Freudian or Jungian orientated counsellor or analyst is less likely to be willing to answer the direct questions, whereas a humanistic or person-centred counsellor may feel that it is fine for the client to have some personal information right at the outset.

Exactly what is said will, of course, depend on what the client asks, and how the counsellor responds will depend not only on the original counselling orientation but also on the counsellor's experience of telephone work. The counsellor must be clear about what questions would be permitted, how they would be answered and why it might not be appropriate to answer others. Whatever the counsellor decides with regard to answering personal questions or indeed *offering* personal information, a consistent approach is essential and the counsellor must have prepared the broad content of responses, since hesitation or pauses could be interpreted by the client as unwillingness to answer or the client may feel that they have asked something which the counsellor does not feel comfortable about answering. This could lead to a block before the sessions begin!

To what sort of questions am I referring? The client may be curious about what the counsellor looks like or is wearing or where the counsellor is sitting for the session, where they live or are working from. These questions, which in the main would be answered without asking if the two people were face to face, may have to be answered in some way to prevent them becoming blocks to the sessions. Indeed, the counsellor and client may choose to send each other photographs of themselves, perhaps in the place where they sit for the sessions, as a way of addressing this area.

It is perhaps unlikely to be appropriate to answer questions concerning aspects of the counsellor's personal life and relationships, but other issues might be relevant such as whether or not the counsellor has had personal experience of the type of problem(s) presented by the client. Dryden and Feltham (1995) suggest other questions clients might wish to ask potential counsellors concerning the counsellor's areas of speciality, qualifications, working methods, ground rules and the contract. If the client decides to continue after the preliminary session, the first session can begin from a more informed base.

Poor-quality telephone connections

The counsellor should have a strategy for dealing with technical problems – for example if one gets a crossed line part-way through a session, or if the line is not clear – although this may not need to be explicit. In such a case, the counsellor might need to interrupt the session, pointing out why and asking the client to re-dial: 'I don't know if you can hear some noise/crackling on the line, but I think it would be better to put down the receiver and immediately call me again.'

Control

The telephone client clearly has far greater control over the relationship than in a conventional face to face relationship. The most obvious manifestation of this is that the client can choose to end the session at any point by hanging up. This degree of client control can be difficult for the counsellor to accept while being quite liberating for the client.

The reality that a telephone client is theoretically less dependent on the counsellor – it is easier to put down the phone than to walk out of a session – brings with it an equality which may be one reason why I believe that telephone clients seem to be more comfortable with the relationship more quickly than clients who physically visit a counsellor.

Further, the nature of the dependency between the client and the counsellor is quite different from a conventional face to face relationship. By distancing themselves physically and by relying on something else, the telephone, to link them, both the counsellor and the client are more independent and free.

What to discuss is, in some respects, far more the choice of the client than might otherwise be the case. After all, how will the counsellor know whether the client is telling all of the story, or where there might be discrepancies without the visual cues to support or to challenge the words?

Insurance

All counsellors need to protect themselves. Professional indemnity insurance is essential for any counsellor in a regular practice, including those who do telephone work. Telephone helpline services often find that they can add clauses to their general insurance policies to protect those workers who provide information, support or counselling by telephone in the working environment. Individual counsellors might wish to ask their current insurers or insurance brokers for their domestic practices about additional cover in case of claims for breach of professional duty in giving treatment (counselling) or advice by telephone.

It is certainly possible to have professional liability insurance for counselling by telephone, whether done on a one-to-one or on a group basis, by textphone and for counselling by E-mail.

Case Study D
The Spinal Injuries Association, London

One example of an organisation using telephone counselling successfully is the Spinal Injuries Association, the national association for spinal cord injured people, based in North London. The information provided here reflects the practice of the service during its first five years.

The Telephone Counselling Line opened in September 1990. The team of eight professional counsellors working on the Counselling Line are themselves paralysed and have an in-depth understanding of the issues associated with spinal cord injury. While a range of non-directive, non-judgemental approaches is used, the counsellors are able to practise their own distinctive ways of working within this framework. The counsellors are paid on a sessional basis.

Once selected to work for the organisation, all counsellors receive both induction training and ongoing training. The training covers telephone counselling skills, self-awareness, groupwork skills and training in disability and peer counselling issues.

When a caller rings the service, the counsellor makes an assessment of the caller's needs, helping to clarify issues and explore the best way forward. If ongoing counselling is felt to be appropriate, a contract is then agreed.

When a contract is agreed, the counsellor will set the objectives of the counselling and will agree with the client the time, date and number of sessions. When an appointment has been made, the Counselling Line is kept free for the call to be received. The clients generally make the calls and therefore pay for them, but if this is not possible, perhaps due to financial reasons, the counsellors can call their clients.

It may sometimes be more appropriate to make an open contract, whereby the caller is encouraged to telephone the Counselling Line and talk to whichever counsellor is on the line at the time of calling.

THE CONTRACT

The maximum length of each session is 60 minutes. The counselling emphasis is on brief focal work, with short term contracts of up to six sessions and longer term contracts agreed according to the client's needs and situation. All longer term counselling work is discussed in supervision with the manager of the service and the counselling objectives are re-assessed in line with the organisation's boundaries of telephone work.

TRAINING, SUPPORT AND SUPERVISION

The Telephone Counselling Service is a member of the British Association for Counselling. In accordance with the BAC requirements, all counsellors receive regular supervision of their work. Individual telephone supervision with the service manager takes place within a day of each session and there is a monthly training programme, part of which includes face to face group supervision for all the counsellors.

Supervision is generally focused on the counsellor's assessment of the client and on the interactions in the counselling relationship.

CASE NOTES

The only records kept are for monitoring purposes and all counsellors are required to maintain confidential case notes.

Clearly, for the Spinal Injuries Association, in offering peer counselling the counsellors' own experiences are considered to be vital to enable them to empathise with the clients. It is essential, therefore, that the counsellors are very comfortable with their own disability if they are to work with paraplegic and tetraplegic clients. The supervision that follows on quickly after each session can help to attend to any transference and boundary issues which may arise and helps the counsellor to develop strategies for dealing with them.

The first session

Once the negotiations have been concluded and the arrangements for the timing, the dates and the number of sessions before a review takes place have been agreed, the client will then know when next to call the counsellor for sessions to begin.

Many counsellors will have experienced the client who starts the first session (at least!) with 'I really don't know what to say, to fill up the time' and who then promptly talks non-stop for 40 minutes or so. This may sometimes apply to the telephone too, but it is less common, since without the physical presence and because the client is not able to see the counsellor's reactions, or lack of them, the first few sessions can be experienced as unnerving and can lead to hesitancy. The client needs to know, therefore, that the counsellor is still there and has not gone to sleep or off to make a drink or is being distracted by something else. Indeed, it is the counsellor's responsibility to ensure that the client is aware of the counsellor's presence with verbal gesturing or an occasional reflection or open question.

A sigh or a yawn from the counsellor can sound greatly exaggerated and the client is also likely to hear any covering of the telephone mouthpiece, which might be to hide a sigh or a yawn, but could be also interpreted by the client in any number of other ways: who else is there? are they listening in? am I boring the counsellor? why is my counsellor not listening to me properly? It would take a very bold client to dare to ask any of these questions of the counsellor in the first session – if ever – so the counsellor must be totally honest with the client if the mouthpiece is to be covered and say why.

Apart from learning to be really aware of how the client might possibly perceive such actions, the counsellor needs to be aware of what is heard after making an interjection, paraphrase, reflection, question or verbal gesture. Does the client respond? Does the client seem to ignore the intervention? These are all vital components to aid the counsellor's understanding of the client and the beginnings of the working relationship.

Having to think explicitly about things one generally takes somewhat for granted with a client can take practice, patience and an increased level of self-awareness and different style of behaviour for the counsellor. Indeed, in the first session with a new client the counsellor might be largely concerned with these levels of operation and perception, rather than really taking in all that the client is talking about. This does not belittle the significance of the client's words, but is more a measure of how the working relationship has to develop when totally dependent on the telephone. In time, perhaps after a couple of sessions, the words can take greater priority as the counsellor's interpretations of non-verbal responses become more intuitive.

These non-verbal levels of awareness can be different for different clients, hence the need to establish what constitutes 'normal' for each client separately. Indeed, telephone counselling is an excellent way of reminding counsellors of the importance of not making assumptions or jumping to 'label' or categorise clients.

Finally, the counsellor should be aware of the time throughout the session, in order to ensure that a clear ending can take place. As outlined in Chapter 2, this requires the counsellor to alert the client that the session is nearly over, perhaps when there are three to five minutes left. The counsellor might need to be directive to ensure that the session will end on time 'as we won't be able to discuss _____ this session, I wonder if there's any last thing you want to add this time. . . .' It is worth noting that some clients can feel really angry at such a forced ending, but since the time boundary must be kept in the majority of counselling relationships, this can only be addressed in subsequent sessions and it might be a case when the counsellor introduces the subject rather than waiting for the client to do so.

Effective handling of emotions

Emotional outpourings can be hard to contain or to work with on the phone. It is not possible to offer a literal tissue to the client, and sitting holding on to a receiver listening to sobs can take some getting used to.

Counsellors may feel impotent in such situations, and simply saying 'It's OK, I'm still here, take as long as you wish', to a client who is finding it difficult to speak, can lead to frustration, particularly if the counsellor is not very experienced in telephone work. This needs careful management during the session and should be worked on after the session by the counsellor at supervision. The telephone equivalent of offering a tissue can be carried out with a careful tone of voice rather than many words. The sickly sweet, patronising tone some people adopt when talking to a pet or a child is not going to be the most suitable for a distressed adult; nor is a brisk, efficient, 'I'm in control' tone which can be heard as sharp and uncaring. A warm, empathic tone is needed, one which conveys 'I am not being fazed by your emotion – I can take it and I can still be here for you when you feel ready.' Counsellors new to telephone work could find it helpful to practise by tape recording their own voice and hearing how it sounds to themselves and to others (see also counsellor vocal quality, below). Few people like the sound of their own tape-recorded voice, but with telephone counselling your voice and how you use it can literally make or break the relationship with clients, so tape recording during training and afterwards for occasional self-monitoring is essential.

Anger can be very much easier for a client to express on the phone. This might be partly because the client can't see the counsellor and can therefore focus on her or his own needs without being concerned about how the counsellor might react to the anger. Again the counsellor will have to be able to allow and work with the emotion and be clear not to get caught up in any transference or inappropriate displacement of this anger on to the counsellor. This is not to say that a counsellor has to tolerate personal abuse, torrents of swearing or intense, uncontrolled anger where this is not the known behaviour of the client although the counsellor should stay with the call for long enough to try to perceive what is going on for the client and to try to convey this or work with it. It might be appropriate to terminate such a call however and this can be done by stating directly that that is what is going to happen: 'You are clearly very angry about _____ I cannot work with you unless you can tell me more about it.' Pause to see if the client responds. If not, 'I am not prepared to listen to continued raging, so I am going to terminate this call.' At which point the counsellor then hangs up. Clearly what happens next, in terms of who calls whom and when, will depend on the original contract. Incidentally, if this exchange occurs in a one-off helpline situation, the caller may ring back later or not and the worker will need to take time out to calm down or unwind before taking another call, but it is not generally appropriate for any helpline worker to be abused by a caller.

On the other hand, a passive-aggressive or a 'yes, but' client can transfer anger, which may be impossible to express otherwise, to the counsellor who must then decide whether or not to respond in an explicit way, by exploring the client's feelings or reflecting their own feelings to the client.

In general, being honest about what is being perceived is probably the best policy for the telephone counsellor. 'I'm not sure but it seems as if . . .' can be a safe way of approaching this, leaving the client with the option of being able to correct the counsellor if need be.

Talking about sex

Just as the phone can be liberating for clients, enabling them to express strong emotions, so it can also give clients the freedom to talk about sex and sexual issues that they might not address as readily in a face to face situation. Counsellors must be able to respond and to work with what the client brings in a depth and manner that may be quite different from that required in face to face sessions.

The telephone can also provide clients with the opportunity to make inappropriate sexual inferences or suggestions to the coun-sellor. How to respond to these will depend on the relationship which has been established between the client and counsellor. Even with a relatively new client it might be important that the counsellor responds in a constructive manner 'It sounds as if there is something important to be discussed behind what you are saying. Can we find another way of talking about it?'

Changes in circumstance

Sometimes a face to face client might become a telephone client, perhaps because they move to live farther away. The change from one medium to another has to be addressed; this change in circumstances will have an impact on the sessions. It is perhaps advisable to end the original contract and then negotiate a new one, by phone and for the phone. In some ways this change of medium can be relatively easy and certainly there is less scope for fantasy or misdirected imaginings with a client one has previously seen and got to know.

There may be good reason to hold both telephone sessions and a few face to face sessions with a client, in which case the counsellor should be aware of, and openly discuss and work with, any differences in the sessions which may be due to the changing medium.

It is important to be clear about the reasons for mixing the media and the possible outcome or impact this has on the counselling process. For example, it might be the case that emotions are only expressed during telephone sessions or that the client is always late for the face to face sessions but on time for the telephone sessions. If such issues are encountered, the counsellor will need to address these with the client in some way compatible with the counsellor's counselling orientation, in order to be clear whether the behaviour is linked to the medium or to the counselling process. Should it be found that the client is not as comfortable with one medium or the other, this can be redressed. If the behaviour is linked to the process of counselling, this, of course, can be worked with as it would be in any type of counselling session.

Case Study E
The CareAssist Group Limited – EmployeeCare

EmployeeCare is one example of an employee assistance pro-gramme (EAP) which provides counselling by telephone and face to face. Although passing reference will be made to the face to face work, the primary reason for including this case study is to highlight how telephone counselling is carried out by one of the most experienced commercial *telephone-based assistance services in the UK. CareAssist, which is a member of the Royal Insurance Group, has operated telephone services for legal matters since 1979. The employee assistance counselling programmes have been operating since 1990 and grew out of the awareness of the limitations of the legal service, in so far as it could not address all aspects of the issues brought by its callers.*

The service is available 24 hours a day, 365 days a year and the first point of contact for any caller is a telephone 'receptionist', who answers the call and then passes the caller on to a counsellor as appropriate. The 'receptionist' or control room staff have to ensure that the caller belongs to a company which is contracted to use the service, or is a family member of such an employee, and then establishes whether the caller requires legal advice or counselling. If counselling is required, the caller is passed to a counsellor who is on-site and takes the call then and there.

There are approximately 30 counsellors and lawyers who are available on a rota basis covering the lines and staffing levels are varied according to demand. They are backed up by approximately 10 sessional counsellors who provide cover for these full-time employees.

If a call is received and all the counsellors are busy, there is a one-hour guarantee to the caller that a counsellor will return their call or that they can ring in again at a specific time within the hour and a counsellor is guaranteed to be available (for information, this time guarantee is 20 minutes for legal calls). Generally, unless there has been a critical incident in a company, the quietest period for calls is between midnight and the morning and so there might be only three counsellors on duty during this period.

If face to face counselling is considered by both the telephone counsellor and the caller to be the most appropriate follow-up after a telephone call, the caller is linked to a counsellor who is near to them. There are 540 associates around the UK to take up this work.

All telephone counsellors and associates are paid and are required to have specialist knowledge in areas of work as well as having counselling qualifications and counselling experience. The organisation seeks to have a range of counsellors from different social and cultural backgrounds as well as different counselling orientations.

CONTRACTS

The telephone counselling service has no limits on the number of sessions a client might have. The face to face service, however, does not provide long term counselling or therapy and the exact number of sessions each caller is able to have depends on the contract CareAssist has with the company using the service. This is generally between five and eight sessions per employee.

No telephone counsellor is permitted to take on more than 22 hours per week counselling and indeed many do not do more than 18 hours' counselling. The rest of their time is spent on case notes and case discussion, training, peer support and supervision.

While sessions might last for up to 50 minutes, if the caller has finished all that she or he wants to say in 35 minutes, the session will end then by mutual agreement. The counsellors have found that sessions early on in a course of counselling are more likely to go for the full time, whereas later on they seem to be briefer with an estimated overall average call length of 38 minutes.

Callers may ring to talk to their counsellor at an agreed appointment time if this fits in with their work schedules and if they wish to do so. Otherwise they can ring in at a time when they know their counsellor is on duty, although they might not be able to talk to their counsellor immediately, if the counsellor is talking to someone else.

As was stated earlier, the service is available not only to the employee of the particular company which contracts the service but also to the employee's family. Usually the telephone counselling takes place one to one, but occasionally where face to face work is not possible for whatever reason, couples are counselled with the partners each taking one telephone extension.

CASE NOTES

It is important that people using the service know that what they talk about with their counsellor is confidential and that their employers are not going to be given any detail about the sessions. The counsellors keep their own case notes which are to be objective and brief, detailing only the counsellor's interventions. Case notes are not otherwise identifiable to any particular client, further preserving confidentiality.

TRAINING, SUPPORT AND SUPERVISION

A heavy emphasis is placed on the selection and recruitment of counsellors. Ongoing training is provided which may be related to specific issues such as child sexual abuse. The counsellors are expected to be able to adapt their own specific theoretical models to work in an eclectic way to meet each client's different needs. It is important that counsellors are not afraid of active intervention in so far as making suggestions and discussing options with callers is concerned.

Supervision for the telephone counsellors is provided in a face to face setting by an external, local supervisor. The associates retain their own counselling supervisors and have supervision either by telephone or face to face by chartered clinical psychologists from the Maudsley Hospital.

The service manager, Sandra Ridley, herself a trained, experienced counsellor and supervisor, is also available for staff support. Sandra believes that counsellors new to telephone counselling need a great deal of support when they first start to work for the service: 'one can't prepare them for the intensity and speed of [what happens] when you put skilled counsellors on the end of a phone, until they do it'.

Counsellor vocal quality

How the counsellor actually sounds can have a big impact on how the client responds. Some research has been conducted – relating to English (Canadian) voices – by Rice and Kerr (1986) which examines ways of measuring what it refers to as 'Client and Therapist Vocal Quality'.

An analogue therapy study using Interpersonal Process Recall (IPR) ratings enabled a sample of 28 client/therapist pairs and over 500 responses to be considered in terms of clients' direct feedback on their perceptions of their therapist's understanding, helpfulness and discomfort. The effect of the therapist's vocal quality on the client was assessed by the client and an analysis was made of what functions were carried on in 'good therapy'.

In 'good therapy', the therapist can affect the client in three ways: through communication of the therapist's state, by modelling a process by which material can be explored and through the interpersonal messages contained in the interaction.

Seven therapist vocal qualities were defined:

1. *Softened* – adequate energy with relaxed vocal muscles producing a soft voice which conveys involvement and intimacy;
2. *Irregular* – the pace and pitch vary;
3. *Natural* – adequate energy, standard English emphasis patterns conveying interest with neither too much tension nor too relaxed a voice;
4. *Definite* – full, measured, assured and can sometimes sound overbearing. Has medium or high energy;
5. *Restricted* – adequate energy for the content, but strained. Comes across as uninvolved, held back, whiny or droning;
6. *Patterned* – Patterned for emphasis and particularly for pitch. Where at the end of a phrase pitch would usually go down, it rises or is level. Sounds 'sing-songy';
7. *Limited* – low energy or flatness. Voice is too soft or too high and squeaky. Can be a monotone and comes across as quite lifeless.

'Good therapy' was defined as containing softened, irregular and natural categories. The 'softened' category applies when a therapist is building a relationship with the client – encouraging trust and implying safety. An 'irregular' component will be displayed during exploration and when the therapist is seeking to understand or find meaning in what the client is expressing. A regular conversational tone, the 'natural' category, is used by the therapist when working with what has been discovered.

It follows then that the 'limited' category is unhelpful as it does not convey interest and the 'restricted' category is likely to be too distancing for the client to feel the therapist's involvement.

This leaves the 'patterned' and 'definite' categories. The 'patterned' category can block expressiveness and exploration or convey a lack of sensitivity, while the 'definite' category can block the client from disagreeing with the therapist.

This is only a précis of the study, but illustrates how significant is the therapist's voice and the impact it can have on the client, irrespective of any words used. As stated above, the study was conducted for English speakers and the implication is that English is the speaker's first (natural) language. It should be remembered that pitch and tone can have different interpretations in different languages. This suggests that counsellors who work with clients for whom English is not their first language might need to study more closely and be aware of how to respond to the clients' voice tones and patterns in order to work most effectively by telephone.

Telephone work and the patient/doctor relationship

The use of the telephone to follow up patients rather than have them attend for further clinic appointments has been studied and commented upon in the US and UK. Rao (1994), a Consultant in Public Health for Sandwell Health Authority, wrote an article on this subject. However, there is a difference between carrying out follow up work and actually using the telephone for supportive work with patients who might otherwise have to attend clinics. Further, in these days of restricted funding or tight budgets, the telephone can be used very cost-effectively in place of face to face work. Supportive, cost-effective telephone counselling work is illustrated in the following case study.

Case Study F
The Multiple Births Foundation: study to consider the effectiveness of telephone consultations for parents as an alternative to clinic attendances

This is an example of how the telephone can be used to support people and to offer a service which is complementary to a traditional clinical service, acknowledging that its clients have special needs which can make clinic visits difficult. In 1994–5 the Multiple Births Foundation (MBF) conducted a study using 50 families, to see how effective are telephone consultations within an advisory service (see also Read et al., 1996).

The MBF is based at Queen Charlotte's and Chelsea Hospital in London, although twins clinics are also held in Birmingham and York. Further there is a Supertwins (triplets and more) Clinic, a Growth Clinic, a Health Visitor Clinic and a Bereavement Clinic in London.

Although strictly speaking what the telephone service offered was not counselling with a capital 'C', as the study progressed it became apparent that the person dealing with the calls was, in fact, being required to use in-depth counselling skills in some situations and general counselling skills throughout. The worker, Barbara Read who is the MBF Family Services Co-ordinator, was a trainee counsellor during the time of this particular study. Barbara's training was taking place on day release at an established counselling training centre. The training was somewhat eclectic but was based on psychodynamic theories. Apart from her counselling training, Barbara had eight years of experience working in the field of multiple births.

BACKGROUND TO THE STUDY

Dr Elizabeth Bryan, an experienced paediatrician, founded the MBF in 1988 to provide professional care for families with twins, triplets or more. A strong focus of its work has always included the use of the telephone to help parents and professionals and with funding received from the Joseph Rowntree Foundation, a specific Telephone Consultation Service was established in 1994. The project was evaluated during and after a year by Ann Condy (1995) of the Family Policy Studies Centre.

The study arose directly from clients' expressed needs, since parents would often ring the MBF with enquiries and to talk about anxieties and stresses. In addition, twins clinics were overloaded with non-medical problems such as relationship issues, schooling, language, sleep and behaviour problems. To address this, evening meetings were set up for parents, but these clearly excluded some parents because of a geographical bias. The aims of the study were, therefore 'to assess the value and efficacy of a professional telephone advisory service as an alternative, where appropriate, to a clinic consultation, thereby making the services of the MBF available, effectively and economically both for the MBF and for clients, to a larger number of people from a wider geographical area, and to develop a model which may be used, with necessary safeguards, by other caring agencies'.

The telephone project sought to 'filter out' parents who did not really need a clinic appointment and offer them the choice of three other options. First, callers to the MBF were able to speak to a specific worker, Barbara Read, who would work with the caller as far as possible within her personal and professional boundaries. Secondly, Barbara referred more complex calls, which were essentially medical in nature, to Dr Bryan for a telephone consultation or to another member of the medical staff as appropriate. Thirdly, parents were offered a clinic appointment if it was felt necessary or if that was what they decided they did want at the end of either their call with Barbara or following the telephone consultation with Elizabeth Bryan.

THE PROJECT

Barbara was available four days a week from 9 a.m. to 3 p.m. for callers, the fifth day being spent at college, when emergency cover was available from Dr Bryan or another experienced medical staff member. Barbara had monthly supervision from a staff counsellor and management supervision from Dr Bryan.

Barbara explains that initially she found she was referring not only medical cases to Dr Bryan for her telephone consultation sessions, but also parents whose concerns were with their children's sleep patterns, eating difficulties and some behaviour issues. Another member of the team, the director of administration and professional education, would talk on the phone with parents whose concerns were related to school places and appeals against decisions in this area. As her confidence grew, Barbara was able to deal effectively with many of the calls about sleep patterns or aspects of child behaviour. When she looked closely at her techniques, she found that she was in fact tending to use a person-centred approach in her work. Barbara could call the parent back rather than have them run up large phone bills if the parent indicated that the worry about the cost of the call might prohibit them from talking to her.

Those parents who had telephone consultations with Dr Bryan were allocated appointments to ring the office for up to 20 minutes on one of two evenings per month. Unless there were clearly financial difficulties, the parents paid the cost of the call to Dr Bryan. Barbara allocated the appointments and had already talked with the parents so was able to brief Dr Bryan with sufficient background for the latter to conduct an effective session and the parent did not have to repeat everything.

Many of the calls which Barbara received required her counselling skills and support. Many callers needed to talk and express their fears of not being good enough or they felt that their partner was not doing things adequately. It may be that for such callers the anonymity of the telephone was a big incentive to call. For others, attending clinics required them to travel long distances with their children, so the telephone was a helpful and less expensive option.

RESULTS OF THE STUDY

Who called?
Mostly it was found that mothers called – 63.3 per cent of the calls, compared with only 4.7 per cent of fathers – the rest of the calls being from professionals, or from other family members, both parents together or an adult twin.

Geographical location of callers and twins
83.2 per cent of the twins had been born elsewhere than Queen Charlotte's and while approximately 39 per cent of the callers were local, and over 27 per cent lived within a 35-mile radius of the hospital, 32 per cent lived beyond this distance.

Speed of having problem addressed and time considerations
The fact that calling the MBF and speaking to Barbara was effective and quick is demonstrated in the findings that 20.9 per cent of all callers cited speed of having their problem addressed as an advantage and almost 26 per cent noted that the advantage of not having to travel was important. About 16 per cent acknowledged that the telephone was far less time consuming than a clinic visit and 15 per cent that it was more convenient simply being able to pick up the phone during the day. Over 7 per cent thought an advantage was the saving in money of a call compared to travel, child care or other costs which might be incurred if a visit took place.

THE COSTS OF THE SERVICE
A paper considering the relative costs of the telephone and clinic services was presented to an International Congress for Twin Studies (Read and Bryan, 1995). MBF staff calculated that the average cost to the MBF of supporting the families by telephone was £10.37 per family. The most expensive of the cases in the study cost the MBF £33.74 and the least expensive cost £0.97. The costs include the cost of staff time.

Of the 50 families in the study, at least 26 would have been offered a clinic appointment before the telephone service existed. All of these lived within a 35-mile radius of the hospital and so would have been expected to attend. Looking at the costs for these 26 families, the average cost of the telephone support was £13.37 with a range of £33.74 to £1.94. To have supported them in the clinic setting would have cost the MBF £51.81 per family, an average saving of £38.44 to the MBF, which is 74 per cent of normal clinic costs.

SUMMARY

Ninety per cent of all callers found Barbara to be very or quite helpful, 1 per cent stated that they had not found her helpful and 9 per cent spoke to a member of staff other than Barbara. In addition, 25 per cent said that they found the call had helped them to cope, with 20 per cent also stating that the call had given them a new perspective and 23 per cent that it had helped them realise they were not alone.

As a result of this study, the project is being continued and while Barbara recognises that there is much to be done to encourage some parents, particularly those from minority ethnic communities, to call, the reduction in clinic overload has been significant and the benefit to parents in the immediacy and the confidentiality of the telephone service has been clearly demonstrated.

Culture and language

There are, of course, cultural barriers to counselling. Counselling is neither appropriate nor is it the most effective method for addressing and working through emotional problems or distress for people from many communities. It is unlikely that the telephone will be any more valuable a tool for these people than face to face counselling would be. Indeed, in some communities the use of and access to the telephone are limited.

Telephone counselling in the UK presents a further, obvious barrier to anyone who does not have good conversational English, unless, of course, the counsellor has fluency in other languages. Similarly, if either the client or the counsellor has a strong accent of any sort, the telephone might not be the most suitable medium for sessions between those two people. Counsellors should be aware of using, or of their clients' use of, local colloquialisms and must be able to explain these or to ask clients to explain any they use which are not clear to the counsellor.

While there are growing numbers of counsellors from many minority ethnic communities, seminars, conferences and meetings of counsellors show that counselling still remains predominantly a white occupation and concern, its services presumably used mainly by white people.

It is important to know that there are still only a few *specific* helpline services for people from minority ethnic communities, compared with several hundred other helplines listed in the directory produced by the Telephone Helplines Association (1996).

There are many factors to take into account when considering why this is the case, but they are beyond the scope of this book. However, it is interesting to note that Baxter (1989) makes clear reference to the different support and information needs of people affected by cancer within different minority ethnic communities compared to cancer support and information needs of white people.

Telephone counselling with deaf clients

It is possible to have counselling sessions with deaf clients if both client and counsellor have access to a textphone, but this may not be the most effective medium for ongoing counselling sessions unless (or even if) the counsellor is fluent in the use of the textphone keyboard and language. The 'Typetalk' service offered by British Telecom (see also Chapter 7) is not an appropriate medium for counselling since it involves a third party, an operator, 'translating' between a client's textphone and the counsellor's ear. This has obvious implications for confidentiality and indeed could be ripe for inaccuracies to sneak in. Further, there will be an inevitable delay in communication between the client and counsellor so spontaneity will be lacking. With both textphone and the 'Typetalk', there is no means by which the counsellor or the client can convey anything of themselves in a non-verbal sense, such as pitch and tone of voice, which, as has already been explored, is an essential part of telephone counselling.

Gender and telephone counselling

Although many helpline services often report that their callers are mainly women, this clearly depends on the subject and nature of the call and perception of the service. It is not very common for callers to ask to speak to a specific gender of counsellor or helpline worker.

Research by Salminen and Glad (1992) in the US found that calls received by female counsellors tended to last longer than those received by male counsellors although the interaction of caller with counsellor gender was not statistically significant. Both female and male counsellors were able to work effectively with male callers when simply listening to their problems but female callers were helped more with empathic understanding. This seems to suggest that counsellor technique is more important to the caller than counsellor gender.

Summary: some of the advantages which telephone counselling can bring compared with face to face counselling

- Counsellor can work with a wide ranging geographic spread of clients.
- Clients can choose a counsellor for reasons other than location, such as choosing one who specialises in a particular subject, has a particular theoretical orientation or is from a particular community or cultural background.
- Counsellors do not have to admit strangers to the home/office.
- Neither party has to travel anywhere.
- Telephone counselling is ecologically efficient, reducing transport pollution and congestion.
- Neither party has to be physically mobile to participate.
- Neither party has to be feeling 100 per cent well to participate.
- There is greater equality between the client and counsellor as the relationship develops.
- The counsellor must constantly check any assumptions made by either counsellor or client.
- The counsellor must be aware of and sensitive to her/his voice patterns and intonations and their possible impact on the client.
- There is less likelihood of abuse by the counsellor, for example in terms of inappropriate social or sexual contact.
- Clients can feel safe to talk more readily about deeply personal issues, emotions and experiences.
- The tradition that counselling takes place on the counsellor's terms is challenged.

6

Telephone Group Work

The concept of running a counselling group by phone is quite new. There is, however, an increasing trend towards working with clients in a telephone group setting. Much of the pioneering work in training people on the telephone to be telephone counsellors has been carried out by Emma Fletcher who worked as a trainer for Phobic Action. Emma developed and conducted a training programme, which was started in 1990, for volunteers who would then provide one to one telephone counselling for people experiencing severe anxiety disorders, in a self-help framework.

Using a variety of techniques adapted from her own practice in face to face group work and previous experience as a Samaritan, Emma carried out training in 12 weekly telephone group sessions, each of one hour's duration, setting homework between sessions which required participants to be paired with each other through telephone contact (Fletcher, 1994).

From my own experience, beginning with the co-facilitation of a telephone support group in 1992 for women who had breast cancer and leading to a second co-facilitated group in 1993 for women who had gynaecological cancer (see Case Study H, below), the telephone group has now become an established part of my working life.

This chapter will introduce the concept and issues to be taken into account in telephone group work. The two case studies in this chapter cover the use of the telephone group as a counselling skills training tool and provide an example of a short term, closed therapeutic counselling group.

Practicalities of group work

There are a number of practical requirements for conducting group work by telephone. Obviously, there needs to be the facility to link up all the participants and the facilitator or group conductor at the same time. The facilitator must be familiar with working with this medium, in order to effectively facilitate and manage the group. This chapter will outline the role of the facilitator and consider how such groups might work.

Conference call facilities can be arranged through a telecommunications company or through organisations like Community Network, a charity which can link people together in a conference call charging special rates for self-help and support groups. Community Network only accepts bookings from charities and not-for-profit organisations.

Before the group begins

It can be helpful for the facilitator to speak briefly to each potential group member before the sessions begin to talk through how the linking up of the participants will happen and to mention other practicalities of participation which are addressed on subsequent pages. It is not appropriate for the client and counsellor to discuss any other issues which could otherwise come out during the group sessions.

When running a counselling or support group, it is important not to have too many participants, to ensure that all have a good chance of joining in. Having a group of no more than eight people with a facilitator who is comfortable with the medium will provide space for participants to work and reflect in an hour-long conference.

The facilitator must decide in advance how long each session will last and should inform the participants so that they can ensure that they are available. An hour in this setting can feel a long time to new participants, but shorter periods are not advisable for therapeutic work. Sessions can be pre-booked for longer, in half-hour segments, should the facilitator wish to do this.

It can take as little as five minutes to bring all the participants 'on line'. This assumes that all participants are available to come 'on line' at the first attempt at contact; if a participant is being contacted through a work switchboard or is not waiting by the phone, it can of course take longer to complete the conference and for the session to begin. Regardless of how long it takes to start, the facilitator should allow about five minutes for a clear ending, so the hour might be more like a 50-minute hour in terms of less formally structured group discussion time.

Linking up

Apart from the obvious need to arrange for everyone to be available by a phone at the appointed time, all the other practical conditions for clients outlined in Chapter 5 need to be ensured.

Background noise in a group session is very intrusive to the session and all participants must have an undisturbed place and space. Telephones with a 'hands free' or loudspeaker facility may be fine to use but cordless phones and mobile phones are not generally suitable in terms of guaranteed signal or line strength and background interference.

If using Community Network, that organisation's operators can dial out to call participants at the appointed time, or participants ring in to one of their special switchboard numbers. If Community Network dials out, a method of payment for the cost of each participant's phone call needs to be agreed beforehand between the facilitator and the participants. It follows that when participants ring in to the switchboard, they pay their own call costs, but the cost of using the conferencing facility will have to be met in some way. The actual call charges themselves are dependent on the time of day, the duration of the call and the distance of the call, that is, where the participants are in relation to the conference facility being used (Community Network has several teleconferencing sites around the UK).

Conducting the sessions

The facilitator has to be interactive to some degree, holding the callers with general conversation until all participants are 'on line'. Then the facilitator may be required to initiate some discussion at the first session, as it is likely that the medium will feel strange.

One generally unthreatening way to start is to ask participants to introduce themselves, however they wish, perhaps saying something about the room in which they are sitting for the call. This enables the group to hear each other's voices, to identify a voice with a name, and it gives everyone the chance to speak.

The facilitator also has to explain some ground rules. Perhaps the most important requirement of which the facilitator must be aware, for at least the first few sessions, is that all speakers must identify themselves by name when they speak. After three or four sessions, people can often recognise each other's voices and this practice may not need to continue.

It is also important to ensure that all participants are offered the opportunity to speak and that no one takes over the whole session. While in a face to face group this may not always be a role of the facilitator, on the phone the facilitator may have to play a more active part in bringing some structure to the group, particularly in the early sessions.

At least initially this need for structure might require the facilitator to have to be more directive than perhaps would be the case in a face to face group, in order to get the group going. Clearly this will not suit all counsellors or counselling orientations.

As the group settles, the facilitator will probably begin to move more towards linking themes or reflecting and summarising issues. In other words, the facilitator's role will change as the participants begin to ask questions or challenge each other, making links, reflecting back to each other and identifying with issues. At this stage, it is even possible that the facilitator may be required mainly to keep time and perhaps help to draw in a silent member or to contain a dominant member. Some groups reach this point by the end of the second session!

The next session may require a bit of a kick-start by the facilitator, but then things should take off and the sessions have lives of their own, relationships building up and interactions happening spontaneously.

Silences in the telephone group setting can be very hard for people to get used to; often someone cuts in saying, 'Is anyone out there?' or, 'Has the equipment failed?' Indeed a several-second silence can feel more like several minutes and it seems that the group setting can encourage more silences than does a one to one telephone counselling session, as people are unsure when to talk, how to come in, or may be anxious not to talk too much in case they 'take over' and dominate the group. Here again, it is not uncommon for a group member to take on a parenting role, looking out for the quieter person or holding back to give more of a chance for others to speak. Unless this is happening in an established and experienced group, when it may be that another group member would pick up on this behaviour, it is likely to be the role of the facilitator to take responsibility for pointing this out and for 'controlling' the management of the group.

It can be helpful for the facilitator, with an eye on the clock, to cut in and tell the group when there are only five minutes left, in order that a clear ending can take place. The facilitator might summarise briefly and then ask each person to say one thing they are taking away from the session or one thing they would like to say to the group. Then all participants can say goodbye and put down their receivers at the same time.

As telephone group work is quite different from one to one, it may be useful to plan (and book the facilities for) an initial commitment of six weeks, one session of one hour's duration each week. This gives most people long enough to decide if the group and the medium suits them. The group can conduct a review to see whether it wishes to continue and to establish a new contract accordingly.

As has already been suggested, it is not advisable to have a group larger than eight; six is a good number to work with as this allows time and space for everyone within an hour and there are not too many voices to get used to.

Some differences between group work by phone and face to face group work

- While some face to face counselling orientations would not usually permit the facilitator to interrupt or challenge a dominant member, relying instead on the group process and the group members to take responsibility for themselves, this type of short term group work does need help and active participation from the facilitator.

- As with one to one telephone counselling, some people find that they cannot settle to the medium and that working without seeing others is too difficult. Their imaginations, fantasies about others in the group or projections, might get in the way of real work about the issues being raised. Experienced groups, however, should be able to accommodate some open exploration of fantasies and projections.

- The group members simply might not gel or one person is very dominant and this may not be challenged, in which case people may not be 'available' for future sessions when they are called or are expected to call in, or they may actively opt out.

- Absences need to be addressed. Even after just one session, if a client does not attend for the next group, other participants will be affected by this and time must be given to exploring how members feel. The intensity and speed of establishing the telephone group bonds cannot be compared exactly to those of a face to face group.

- Among the advantages of this medium are that it does enable people to be linked together with no consideration of their geographical location and can enable specific groups to be run for people who appear to have similar presenting issues.

- The anonymity which the medium provides in terms of participants only having to reveal what they want to, together with the fact that each participant is unlikely ever to meet anyone else from the group, often leads to a sense of trust and a feeling of safety becoming established quite quickly. This is significant for it leads to in-depth counselling far sooner than generally occurs with the average, new, face to face group.

- It can be easier for people to feel able to challenge each other in this medium than if face to face.

- An hour might seem a long time for a phone call, but it provides time enough for all to have the chance to speak and for some issues to develop. Many people remark that they are amazed at how quickly an hour passes and the facilitator giving a five-minute warning and encouraging an ending is vital, creating a clear boundary.

- A telephone group does not require a great time commitment in terms of travel in addition to the session and can therefore be an attractive option for people with many home commitments or who do not wish to go out at night, when many groups run.

- The medium can be very cost effective. Even if the participants are paying the cost of their phone call, as well as a fee to the counsellor, it is rare that an hour long conversation, out of peak charging time, would lead to a total each session as high as the cost in time and money of the person travelling to a counselling group.

Co-facilitation

I have run telephone groups alone and with different co-facilitators. There are two particular advantages of co-facilitation over lone facilitation which are worth mentioning: the first is that the facilitators can debrief and co-supervise each other. The second is that, using Community Network, it is possible to take a participant out of the main conference and into a separate 'channel' with one of the facilitators for a few minutes, leaving the other facilitator with the rest of the group. While this will have an impact on the group dynamic, it may sometimes be an appropriate course of action for dealing with a client's particular distress or if there is an issue which it is felt would benefit from some brief, individual attention. The impact on the group of this splitting off can be discussed within the group. Clearly, this should only be an occasional occurrence and if one client regularly sought individual attention, this would need to be further explored.

Supervision

For the facilitators of any therapeutic telephone groups, the need for supervision is as great as it is with any counselling work. If working alone, the facilitator should ensure that supervision takes place at least every three to four weeks. It should be fortnightly with a short term closed group of six or eight sessions.

As can be seen in Case Study G, for a group with two facilitators with a less therapeutic focus, co-supervision by the facilitators is likely to be sufficient. In Case Study H, a therapeutic group, again the two facilitators co-supervised each other, but this might not always be enough or the most appropriate method, so using an external supervisor should be considered. Ideally the supervisor should hold a joint session by teleconference to reflect the medium and the experience of the clients. Even if the supervision is face to face, I believe it is important that it is a joint session for both facilitators, since the therapeutic group work must be considered alongside the facilitators' relationship.

Case Study G
Group training course: Introduction to Telephone Group Counselling Skills

In 1995 a six-week 'Introduction to Telephone Counselling Skills' course, conducted by telephone, was run and participants attended from across the UK.

The aims of the course were: to enable participants to gain an understanding of what is meant by 'telephone counselling skills' based on a brief person-centred approach, and to give them the opportunity to practise using the skills in a telephone group setting.

Numbers were limited to nine on the course and there were two facilitators (Emma Fletcher and myself). The sessions ran from 7 p.m. on consecutive Thursday evenings. We chose a six-week course as it seemed to be a reasonable amount of time to ask participants for the commitment and it would enable a variety of skills to be taught and explored. In the training, weeks 1, 2, 5 and 6 were of one hour's duration and weeks 3 and 4 were each an hour and a half. This made a total of seven hours' group time and sessions were supplemented with 'homework' and handouts.

The participants were eight women and one man, and the geographical range was wide. Bob, Barbara and Lyndia came from London, Caroline was from Birmingham, Linda was from Oxford, Sue from Dyfed, Susan from Nottingham, Ros was from Powys, Pauline was in Cleveland and Emma was in Gloucester. I attended some sessions from London, others from Glasgow, according to where I happened to be working during that time.

Each individual's age was never discussed, although from the discussions which occurred through the groups it would be acceptable to consider the age range of the group as from 30 to 60. Two participants had physical disabilities that were known to the facilitators. At least one group member belonged to a minority ethnic community. Although two participants had the same name, it was agreed that one would be known as Susan and the other as Sue to avoid confusion.

The work backgrounds of the participants included a carers' worker, a worker in a hospital-based parents' support project, the co-ordinator of a rape crisis and sexual counselling service, workers from branches of a foster parents' organisation and a staff member of a welfare department of a commercial company.

Amongst the group, two people had had some counselling skills training, while others had had none, even though some were carrying out work which required a counselling skills approach to some extent.

Starting with a session where the focus was to enable participants to explore the medium and progressing by week 4 into role plays, the course tested the participants' willingness to accept new horizons and the equipment's ability to respond to our needs! The following is a brief outline of the skills covered in the course.

Telephone body language: *letting others know that you are listening with mmms and similar gestures, awareness of how your voice changes and distorts if using a hands-free telephone rather than holding a traditional handset, sensitivity to background noise.*

Active listening skills adapted for the telephone group: *including effective listening and responding in a telephone group, silences on the telephone, use of open questions, recognising feelings, giving feedback, paraphrasing and reflecting.*

Role play: *in two groups of four and five working partly with pre-prepared role plays given by the facilitators in advance and partly using participants' own experiences of client work to role-play the clients. Role plays were in pairs with the other members of the group acting as listening observers.*

Acknowledgement of the isolation of telephone group work: *when the session ends, there's no chatting as you leave a venue or opportunity to socialise. There is a need to end each session clearly as a group and then for each person to have some means of ending for themselves after each session before they go back to the rest of their world.*

Support and supervision needs: *how can these be met by telephone, by individuals or groups?*

Setting up and facilitating a telephone group: *the practical issues to take into account if planning a session or a series of meetings.*

Participants were also asked to monitor themselves through questionnaires and through the role plays they carried out. Following evaluation of this course and taking on board the participants' positive feedback and constructive criticisms, amendments were made for running future courses. The main issue raised from the first course was about the experience of counselling skills which people brought to the course. Some participants commented that they had felt disadvantaged for being in a group with some people who were more experienced at using counselling skills and had at times felt inhibited in the large group. A reason for being in the group for some participants had been to enable them to explore the medium for themselves; for others it was also to see whether the medium could be useful to them in their work.

The facilitators' own counselling styles differ and they learned much from 'observing' each other too. In terms of planning the course, the facilitators had met once and then conducted all planning by phone and spoke to each other after each session as a debrief and occasionally between sessions as appropriate. This worked well and shows that facilitators can work together without having to physically be together.

When running a telephone training group, it is always worth having a few extra exercises prepared in case of the unexpected. In addition, modern technology can sometimes be less than effective! During one session there were technical problems involving the playing of a cassette tape to the group. An additional exercise was inserted to take up the time, the facilitators always having some extra material ready in case the estimated timings of parts of the sessions were not correct. Time estimates did not always work as hoped. In one instance, the timing of the session was far too tight for a particular role-play exercise to be fully run and discussed.

Future courses would ensure that there was longer for role plays and analysis and would split people into groups based more on their past experience of using the telephone and any previous counselling training. The length of sessions would be altered so that the two 1.5-hour sessions were weeks 4 and 5 when all the role plays took place, instead of weeks 3 and 4, leaving the total overall 'live' group time as seven hours. Further, it was felt that the maximum number of participants for future courses should be eight and that a course could run with a minimum of six people.

How rapidly the group settled down and worked well together followed the facilitators' expectations based on their previous experiences, but the willingness to bring personal material happened even more quickly than either had anticipated. Between sessions the participants were able to contact the facilitators for support or to discuss personal issues if they wished. This happened twice and both times the participant chose to inform the group. Clearly, there could be implications for group confidentiality if any participant constantly contacted the facilitators outside of the sessions and indeed the impact of this on the group dynamic for a therapeutic group means that this would have to be discussed in the wider group, the individual participant being encouraged perhaps to seek personal support from elsewhere, in addition.

Some group members knew each other in advance of the course, but they were split up for any small group work and it did not seem to have any impact on the group dynamics based on comparisons with the facilitators' previous experiences of groups where no one knew anyone beforehand.

Already some of the advantages of training in this medium should be apparent. It would be highly unlikely that such a diverse range of backgrounds, geographical locations and experiences would be found in a face to face group. Cost and convenience of access have been mentioned earlier but other advantages include the following:

– Depth of intimacy was rapidly established.
– The group setting seemed to be a great levelling factor as no one had used the medium in this way before.
– The setting seemed to be liberating, even for 'quieter' people.
– The medium seemed to enable people to take risks with their techniques and styles; perhaps any fear of appearing foolish in front of one's colleagues is reduced in the non-visual group.
– In one case, a participant had been ill on the day of the session, but asked to be able to listen in nevertheless. The person would not have been able to attend a face to face session, but did attend most of the telephone session and so did not totally miss out on that week's course work and group experiences.
– For some participants, the telephone group experience seems to aid awareness of their face to face practice.

The main disadvantages of training in this medium are the lack of social time for participants to meet each other informally, as the sessions start and end all together and do not have a break and the fact that people can sometimes hide and avoid joining in or feel inhibited from doing so. In the training arena, with such a short term group, the facilitators need to take responsibility for drawing people in and for being sensitive to different levels of awareness and experience of counselling skills. Facilitators might have to exercise some control over the group, which would be far less of a requirement in the support or counselling group, when participants seem to be more willing to bring each other into the sessions.

On a technical note, when running any groups, I always arrange for the Community Network operator to call out to each participant, rather than asking people to ring in at a set time. There are several practical reasons why this is an advantage for a closed group, even though it incurs a small, additional cost:

- It ensures that people do not have to dial to 'get in' to the conference and perhaps get an engaged tone if others are trying at the same moment, which can be frustrating or can cause anxiety.
- The operator can then be clear about who is on which line and can easily tell who is being affected by any technical problems that arise (these are remarkably few, in my experience).
- It means that only people who have pre-booked can attend, which can be reassuring for confidentiality and for the group dynamic.

Of course, if the group is to be run as a 'drop-in', then all participants have to dial in themselves. In this case, the facilitator has to be very clear, when setting up and advertising the sessions, about how long after the start time of the group people can choose to dial in. It can be very disruptive if, for example, several people are discussing issues together and after 30 minutes another person joins. With new drop-in groups in particular, when people might not call in regularly, it can be hard to know exactly who has chosen to join the sessions and so it can take longer for the group dynamic, confidentiality and trust to be created.

Case Study H
Therapeutic telephone groups: A telephone group
for women who had experienced gynaecological
cancer

Cancerlink is a national charity providing information and support for anyone affected by cancer. The concept of the telephone group fitted in well with one of the organisation's aims of providing emotional support for people with cancer who may have very specific needs. In October 1993, I co-facilitated a telephone group with Liz Urben, both of us at that time being employees of Cancerlink; an account of the experience was published as a booklet (Rosenfield and Urben, 1994).

It was decided to invite women who had experienced gynaeco-logical cancer to participate in the group since this type of cancer is varied and the cancer and/or the treatments can have a huge impact on the emotional and psychological state of the woman affected. At the time of the group it was felt that there was not always enough (if any) support available in treatment centres. In addition, most local cancer support and self-help groups did not have large numbers of women with experience of these cancers, resulting in isolation for many such women.

The group ran for one hour each week, in the evening, for six weeks. It was intended that the group would be mainly self-directed by the women. This means that the facilitators would not bring an agenda to the group, but would let the discussion flow as the women chose. This was largely what happened although, on occasion, the facilitators felt they had to interrupt where one woman seemed to be making excessive demands on the group and others were unable to join in, although some tried and gradually, over the weeks, became more confident about doing this.

Although eight women initially agreed to participate, one dropped out after the first session as the group was not what she felt she wanted. There was always a core of six in attendance all the rest of the weeks except for the last session when all seven were present. Some of the women were receiving treatment for their cancer, others were many years post-initial cancer treatment. The age range of the group was 30–59 and participants attended from their homes as far apart as Devon and Norfolk.

GROUP PROCESS

During the first session most of the discussion was quite impersonal and the (unconscious) aim seemed primarily to be to establish the participants as group members. The second week contained information sharing and some suggestions were offered from members to others based on issues with which they themselves identified. By the third session discussion was very intimate with the women expressing their strength and depth of feelings about their experiences and the emotional, physical, sexual and psychological impact of their cancer. There was some pairing and greater sense of identification of women who shared specific needs, so even within the telephone group setting there is space for particular relationships and deeper levels of empathy to exist between some participants than between others.

The following session was far 'safer' and lighter in tone and atmosphere, with more general discussion and less vulnerability expressed. The fifth session was back to being more intense, even though, or perhaps because, it was known to be the penultimate session, with deep and powerful material being shared and explored. The trigger seemed initially to have been a TV programme which some of the group had seen and which they felt presented a negative view of cancer and survival. They collectively told the others about the programme and all were in agreement that the media were often responsible for exerting a negative influence on people affected by cancer. Indeed, some participants directed anger at what they saw as the irresponsibility of the media in being one-sided and judgemental. The last session was very much an ending, with the participants sharing anxieties about the future and exploring the loss of the group. All the women expressed a desire to continue to maintain contact and to lessen their isolation by exchanging addresses and phone numbers. These were sent out by the facilitators, with participants' permission, after the session ended.

CONCLUSION

All the participants seemed to gain from the experience of sharing and working together over the six-week period. The medium quickly became comfortable even though none of the participants had ever experienced anything quite like it before. One of the women had a hearing impairment and yet found she could participate equally with the others. She was initially encouraged to ask people to repeat themselves if she did not clearly hear what was said, but in fact found she did not need to do this after the first week.

The facilitators debriefed and supported each other immediately each session ended. This was found to be sufficient. The facilitators have some experience of working with face to face groups and so were able to compare their experiences in retrospect. Many aspects of the telephone group do mimic those of the face to face group, but the relationships seemed to build far more rapidly between the participants. This was thought to be because individuals found it very easy and safe to identify with each other's experiences and feelings, though not always in the same pairings or sub-groupings, which must be due in some part to the anonymity and the lack of physical, visual togetherness. There are limitations to what the telephone group can achieve with no non-group 'social' time together and this might be limiting to a longer term group process, although this has yet to be tried.

For this particular group, the feedback from the participants included:

'Enjoyed it, gained a lot and appreciated it.'

'Everybody is in the same frame of mind . . . nice to know it's not just you . . . it does happen to others.'

'Lovely feeling of friendship . . . reassurance. I'm not alone. . .'.

'. . . not met anyone else with ovarian cancer. Nice to hear people a couple of years on and going strong.'

7

Technology and Counselling by Telephone

While it is to be expected that the technological developments carry with them benefits to users of these services, there are also less helpful aspects which could affect the client–counsellor relationship and of which both parties should be made explicitly aware in case it influences their decision to work with this medium.

In this chapter, some areas of technology will be considered because of their impact, positive as well as negative, on the use of the telephone as a counselling medium. Regulatory conditions which might affect a telephone counsellor are mentioned as well as information about equipment which can facilitate the use of the medium.

Confidentiality

Unquestionably the most important area for consideration is that of confidentiality and it should be the responsibility of any telephone counsellor to ensure that the client is fully aware of the potential for there to be breaches of confidentiality, due to technology, before any contract is agreed and sessions commence.

Quite apart from the usual, obvious aspects of confidentiality for a telephone counselling relationship, such as the client knowing that they can talk about issues which the counsellor does not disclose in detail to anyone else, except during supervision and of course except for any circumstances in which the counsellor may be obliged to breach confidentiality, there are specific and less obvious potential breaches of confidentiality for clients due to telecommunications technology.

The impact of these will depend on where the client is when the sessions take place, for example at home or at someone else's home or at work, as well as on who else knows that the client is receiving counselling.

Leaflets entitled *Calling Helplines* produced and updated annually by the Telephone Helplines Association since 1992, have sought to explain, to helplines primarily, the impact of some of the technological developments on aspects of confidentiality and to inform them of the protection needed to enable people to be assured that they can call helplines and retain their anonymity.

The three main areas for consideration – all of which could cause a breach in the client's confidentiality if they choose not to tell others that they are having sessions with a counsellor – are itemised telephone bills, BT caller display equipment and call return services. They are explained further below. More and more telecommunications operators are also providing similar services.

If a counsellor is working from home with a private counselling practice, there are specific confidentiality issues affecting work on the phone. Having a separate telephone line has been mentioned in Chapter 2, but if the counsellor is calling the client, perhaps to amend an appointment, or at any time other than for a pre-arranged session, it might be necessary for the counsellor to use the '141' number withhold code, in case someone other than the client is there to answer the call and has access to caller display equipment. Using the '141' code prevents anyone else at the client's number from knowing the counsellor's number. If a client wishes to keep the fact of their counselling confidential it is important for the counsellor not to breach this in an inadvertent way.

Itemised telephone bills

Most people calling from their own home using telephone services of the major telecommunications network operators, such as BT, mobile phone networks and cable companies, already receive phone bills where some or all calls made from that number are listed on the bill, with the number dialled and the duration and time of the call and cost stated. When the phone bill arrives and another member of the household such as the bill payer looks at it, regular calls to the same number of about 50 minutes' duration are likely to stand out amongst all the other calls listed.

Clearly then, if a client does not wish anyone in the household to know that they are receiving counselling, they must either arrange for the counsellor to phone them, raising, in a different context, the questions discussed in Chapter 5 about who calls whom and the contract and fees, or they must call from elsewhere. A client calling from a place other than home has to ensure that wherever they are they can have privacy and the details of the counselling calls appearing on the telephone bill of *that* telephone are not disclosed to anyone other than the customer (who will receive the bill) and the client themselves.

Caller display equipment

Although perhaps unlikely in the ongoing counselling relation-ship, it is possible that the client may not wish the counsellor to know from where they are calling, in which case they will need to find out whether the counsellor has caller display equipment. If the counsellor does have this facility, the client's number will then be displayed before the call is answered. Callers can protect themselves against this by dialling '141' before the counsellor's number, in which case the counsellor will see 'number withheld' on the display screen. Incidentally, helplines are encouraged by the Telephone Helplines Association to actively publicise the fact that they will not use caller display equipment and will withhold their own number if calling clients back (see call return).

Call return

If the client phoned the counsellor and the phone was not answered and someone else, other than the counsellor, then went to the phone and dialled 1471, an electronic voice could reveal the number from which the call was made, i.e. the client's number. It is important, therefore, that others answering the phone at the counsellor's household/office premises must be 'trained' to be aware that it may not always be appropriate to call back an unrecognised number.

The electronic voice announces that the number of the last call has been withheld or is unavailable only if the client has permanent number withholding on their phone line or has dialled

'141' before dialling the counsellor's number. It may be important for clients to know that this how they can protect their anonymity and phone number. Call return is available on most BT telephones except for calls made from mobile phones and/or from outside the UK, at the time of writing.

BT has sponsored the *Calling Helplines* leaflet since 1993 and early in 1996 set up a series of public education initiatives including a freephone information line, explaining how callers to helplines can endeavour to ensure that their confidentiality is maintained with regard to itemised phone bills and call return. BT is the only telecommunications company which had sought to consult with the Telephone Helplines Association over several years to learn more about the helpline industry's concerns and to endeavour to act to address these or at least to ensure that public education highlights the potential problems for confidential calls. OFTEL, the telecommunications watchdog, has also participated in these discussions. At the time of writing, however, the first ever meetings were being planned between the Telephone Helplines Association, OFTEL and many of the numerous (approximately 150) telecommunications companies now licensed to operate within the UK, in order to seek an industry-wide solution to enable all callers to seek confidential help by telephone without additional anxiety or fear.

Permanent line blocking

BT customers, including those who are ex-directory and therefore unlisted in general telephone books and by Directory Enquiries, can ask BT to withhold their telephone number on all calls made on their line so that there is no need to dial '141' each time. This also means that the number will not be revealed to anyone using call return. This can be done simply by calling BT (free) on 150 and requesting it.

Records, regulatory issues and confidentiality

Records

The Data Protection Act 1984 requires any data users to register the purposes for which they hold personal data, the nature of the data and to whom they may be disclosed. The data user must also comply with the Data Protection Principles for good data protection practice. Private counsellors, agencies which offer counselling, charities and helplines must all be registered if they are holding client details on computer. More information about this, and about exemptions which might apply, can be obtained from the Data Protection Registrar (see Appendix of addresses).

Monitoring calls and regulatory issues
It is important to note that it is prohibited to record a telephone conversation unless either a warn tone is present so that a beep sound is heard by both parties at regular intervals during the conversation or both parties have given permission for recording to take place. This is in line with the Telecommunications Act 1984 and any equipment which might be used for recording, silent monitoring or intruding into two-way live speech calls must be approved by OFTEL (Office of Telecommunications). However, under the terms of a General Variation (NS/V/1235/T/100023) issued in 1995, the equipment providing the warn tones can be disabled without reference to OFTEL provided that the warn tones are replaced by an alternative form of warning (contact OFTEL for more details). For recording or silent monitoring, this can be either a written notice before the call or a warning during the call itself. The warning should inform all parties to the call why the call is being recorded or silently monitored. For calls where an intrusion takes place, a warning before the intrusion is sufficient.

Private counsellors might be able to satisfy the General Variation by asking their clients for permission to record or silently monitor any part of any session.

Equipment for consideration

Headsets
If conducting regular telephone sessions, it might be feasible for the counsellor to use a headset rather than a handset. A range of telephones can be bought which have optional hand or headsets. Apart from not having to hold the receiver for the duration of the session, headsets can block out background noise and are therefore particularly useful for people working in an open office type of environment. For some counsellors, however, headsets remove some of the intimacy of the interaction with the client.

Phone rests
It is possible to buy special phone rests which support the phone on the shoulder, again removing the need to hold the handset. These plastic phone rests have Velcro strips to enable the handset to be attached and the rest itself then sits on the shoulder. An example of this is the rest supplied by Justfax (see Appendix of addresses).

'Hands-free' phones
Having a telephone with a 'hands-free' or loudspeaker facility can be useful, but the quality of the voice being 'received' is not always very good. Indeed, if a counsellor is using 'hands-free' the client may have difficulty in hearing clearly as the sound is often distorted and echoes. Background noise is significantly amplified if a person is using a 'hands-free' facility.

Telephone accessibility issues

Counselling by textphone
The textphone, more commonly known by the brand name Minicom, is slowly becoming used by more helplines as a means of providing a telephone service to deaf people. A hearing counsellor working from home is unlikely to own a textphone, but may encounter one if working for a counselling or helpline organisation.

The textphone is small (approximately 23 cm × 31 cm × 6.5 cm), light and portable. It has a keyboard similar to a type-writer, although the keys are not identical, and a display screen located across the width of the machine, where one would insert a piece of paper on a small portable typewriter. Above this screen are two rubber cups big enough to contain the mouthpiece and the earpiece of the handset of a telephone. It may be charged up through an AC adaptor and then used *in situ* or remote.

Once connected to a client who also has a textphone, the two people can have a conversation in writing. The words appear across the display screen. Some textphones also have a roll of paper, like an old-fashioned till roll, on which the conversation is printed.

Slow until one is familiar with the equipment, the textphone provides the immediacy of a telephone call for a person who is deaf. Some helplines do offer a textphone as part of their regular

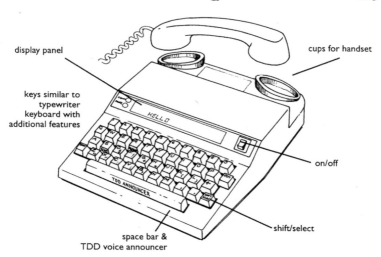

display panel

cups for handset

keys similar to typewriter keyboard with additional features

HELLO

on/off

TDD ANNOUNCER

shift/select

space bar & TDD voice announcer

When the TDD announcer is pressed an electronic voice tells the hearing person to connect their handset to their textphone so that they can receive the call, i.e. it is an audible alert to the hearing person that a textphone user is trying to get through.

ongoing service. Mostly the service is offered on the same telephone number as the regular service, so that it relies on the helpline worker to recognise a textphone call when one comes in. However, few helplines (other than those which work specifically with people who have hearing difficulties or who are deaf) ensure that their workers are fully trained and receive ongoing training for textphone work, which often leads to a less than high quality service for any textphone caller.

There is no reason why a skilled telephone counsellor should not be able to adapt to using a textphone and to holding sessions with deaf clients in this way. This requires training, both in the practicalities of using a textphone and in the type of language used for regular conversation in this medium.

Of course, the medium further limits the clues the counsellor would usually pick up on the phone, from the tone or pitch of the client's voice for example, and therefore might not be very useful for short term work. With more in-depth or long term work it could be a most effective medium because the counsellor would get used to other signs and signals or clues from the client. A distressed or agitated client might type slower/faster/less accurately or use symbols such as !! to emphasise their feelings; only by building the relationship over a period of time would a hearing counsellor be able to use these clues and work with them.

Typetalk services

BT offers a service to textphone users whereby specially trained operators act in a similar way to interpreters, receiving the textphone messages on their own textphones and using their voices to convey the message to a third party, and vice versa. For agencies or counsellors which do not have a textphone, this can offer a link for someone who is hard of hearing or deaf which might not otherwise be possible without using a textphone.

The most obvious disadvantage of using this facility for counselling is clearly the involvement of the typetalk operator, an unrelated third party, in the sessions. Not only does this raise huge confidentiality issues, but it also reduces the spontaneity of the interaction between client and counsellor.

Telecommunications technology is moving rapidly. Even between writing this book and publication some things will have changed, no doubt. The agencies mentioned in this chapter are all useful sources of information about developments. Any counsellor or agency offering a confidential telephone service to the public must take responsibility to keep themselves aware of changes and to inform their clients or potential clients.

8

Counselling by Other Media

Although this book is mainly about counselling and the tele-phone, it would be short-sighted to exclude other media which have been used for providing counselling for some time or indeed are being developed as technology advances. Different media require different approaches, and flexibility for counsellors is essential if they are to rise to and meet the challenge of working with clients in different settings. Indeed, some of these media might encourage people to seek counselling who otherwise would not have contemplated talking through their feelings, problems or concerns with anyone else.

Counselling by letter

It was mentioned in Chapter 3 that CRUSE Bereavement Care offers counselling by letter (see Wallbank, 1994). A number of telephone helpline services may supplement their calls with written information or receive and respond to letters which may be of a counselling/emotionally supportive nature. There are many skills involved in conducting a written counselling relation-ship, particularly one in which there is or has been no other contact between the two parties such as a telephone conversation or a physical meeting. There should be written guidelines to follow if letter counselling is happening in the context of an organisation, where the boundaries and limits of the service must be clearly stated. It should be remembered that the written word can be used as legal evidence and anyone undertaking counselling by letter should be very clear about what they write, how it is written and how it might be interpreted.

For an individual counsellor there are a number of issues to consider if contemplating a written relationship with a client. The following are just a few for starters:

– Both counsellor and client must be reasonably literate and comfortable with the medium.
– A contract must be agreed between them which clearly sets out the framework and boundaries within which they will work, such as number of letters per month, payment of any fees and what issues might be covered (if appropriate).
– It should be decided whether the letters will supplement any other counselling, such as telephone sessions.
– The client should be aware of what happens to any letters sent to the counsellor. Does the counsellor guarantee confidentiality and exactly what does this mean in this context?
– The counsellor should check that the client will be the only person who will open the counsellor's letters, or if this cannot be guaranteed and this is an important issue for the client, whether there is a 'safe' address which can be used instead.
– If there is no visual or aural contact, is it ever appropriate for photographs to be exchanged? Why/why not?
– Can the client send drawings, prose or other material to the counsellor as part of the letter? Why/why not?

When the counsellor receives a client's letter, she or he should allocate specific time, as if a telephone or face to face session were taking place, to work on the letter and a reply, bearing in mind that replying to a letter can take far longer than a therapeutic 50-minute hour. Reading between the lines and being aware of the need to check out assumptions are part of the process of answering the client. As with other forms of counselling there should be acknowledgement of feelings expressed or suggested and letters must be replied to with empathy. It is essential to remember that after writing the letter, the client may not keep a copy and may well 'move on' emotionally – the very act of putting pen to paper can be cathartic – and the reply from the counsellor should indicate some awareness of this. As mentioned in Chapter 4, cognitive-analytic therapists use written communication with clients as part of the therapeutic process and often utilise a 'goodbye letter' at the end of the work. Some employee assistance counselling programmes also offer the option of written contact with the client.

There are other practical issues to explore when counselling by letter, such as how the client first makes contact with the counsellor and how the contract is negotiated: often this will be by telephone. This then leads to the question of why choose letter over telephone for the ongoing sessions?

On the other hand, a client might feel shy or too anxious to initiate contact with a counsellor in any other way than by letter. In this case the counsellor might, over time, discuss using different media with the client to see whether the client might wish to move gradually to face to face or telephone counselling.

As with telephone counselling, not all counsellors are likely to find the letter a good medium with which to work. There are many unknowns which may not be able to be explored, the reply can take a long time to construct – often far longer than a face to face session would take; the counsellor has to be very careful not to make assumptions in the face of the unknowns; and the time span between the client writing and sending the letter, and the counsellor reading, replying and posting the response can be such that the client's circumstances or needs might have changed . . . and how does the counsellor address this?

Counselling by E-mail

On 14 July 1994, Suicide Counselling by E-Mail was launched as a pilot scheme by The Samaritans on the Internet. The E-mail service was initially operated from The Samaritans' Cheltenham branch and operates under the same clear codes that all Samaritans' branches operate of confidentiality and of the right of the caller to make their own decisions, including the decision to end their life. Correspondence is sent through the Internet system to the branch and all contacts receive a reply within 24 hours. Following a very successful first six months, during which over 200 'calls' were received, and after careful evaluation, a second Samaritans' branch, Bracknell, became linked to the Internet and a few other branches are also developing this facility.

It is important to note that while The Samaritans guarantees confidentiality, it is not responsible for the confidentiality of the E-mail system. The Samaritans' modem receiving the Internet correspondence is able to detect unauthorised attempts to read messages, however, so any attempt at tampering should be picked up, and by Spring 1995 no attempted tampering had taken place. As Simon Armson, Chief Executive of The Samaritans points out: 'It has been claimed, with some authority, that the security of confidential messages sent through the Internet is even greater than the security of the telephone, which clearly suits the ethos of The Samaritans.'

With this service, people can contact The Samaritans for help from anywhere in the world, without the receiving branch even knowing from which country the person is making contact, by using a charge-free facility in Helsinki.

It seems clear that for some people the Internet provides a safe and congenial medium to express their feelings and might appeal to people who would not choose to visit a counsellor or even to telephone for counselling. Doubtless, other telephone helpline services will follow suit in time, offering support and perhaps counselling in this medium.

Radio

Many radio stations provide telephone phone-in programmes, but these are generally for comment rather than counselling. Some programmes do, however, use themes or topics which encourage callers who want to talk about something personal in an emotional, social or medical context. What is interesting is how often the caller seems to forget that there are other listeners hearing them pour out their problems to the presenter. The impact on other listeners is not documented, but my own reaction is sometimes one of embarrassment, in which case I switch off, or voyeurism, in which case I listen and then feel uneasy at doing so. Listening to how the caller is heard and responded to by the presenter is, on the other hand, fascinating. Some empathy will usually be expressed and perhaps a few questions, more often than not closed and for qualification rather than for encouraging deeper exploration. Often directive in style, presumably to shorten the on-air time, advice (as opposed to counselling) is given liberally. Clearly with such little time to delve into an issue, counselling as such cannot take place and many calls are more akin to the information-based (as opposed to counselling skills orientated) helplines in style, giving information and directing callers to other options for further help.

Television

Television creates a different dimension again and it is possible to achieve more counselling-orientated responses. There have been various, often late-night, series about relationships and sex and sexuality and even a series in 1995 about family therapy at primetime viewing. Perhaps the influx of American talk shows showing people being very explicit about their problems has made the concept of TV counselling more acceptable to a stereotypically less emotional and less forthcoming UK audience. The voyeurism involved in watching TV therapy somehow seems to me to be different from radio phone-ins, presumably because both parties are visible and it is easier to observe and disengage from the events in this forum.

In his book *The Dryden Interviews* (1992), Windy Dryden, the author interviews Dr John Cobb about his experience of counselling on television. On the programme *A Problem Aired* for Thames Television, John Cobb worked with two clients per programme, each interview lasting 10 minutes initially; later this was changed to working with one client for 20 minutes. The programme was a late-night programme and people applied to be participants. Researchers for the programme would follow up those who wanted to appear and carry out a preliminary selection after talking to them on the phone, in the studio and with relatives.

The aim was to find people who had an 'identifiable, focused problem' and the people had to have 'some degree of physical presentability'. John Cobb would interview the person on the programme, illustrating what could be achieved with a time-limited, general psychotherapeutic approach with cognitive-behavioural goals.

While John Cobb himself stated he would prefer to have longer sessions, he appreciated that there had to be compromises to the medium, in terms of the length of time the session could run before a commercial break. Perhaps even more importantly, he decided as time went on to try to ensure all the clients received some feedback. They were given a tape of the session and were invited to listen to it and return with comments the next week. This opportunity for the client to reflect on the session was a significant extension of their on-air experience, which otherwise seemed to emerge informally after the session had ended. As part of the whole process, this feedback was considered to be an important development.

Thames Television ceased to exist in the early 1990s and so did this form of counselling on TV, although Channel 4 has periodically run counselling-orientated late-night studio discussions.

The videophone

Here is a medium which could be a very good way of offering counselling. It combines aspects of both face to face and telephone work, since the communication channel is through a telephone line but both parties can see each other. Although not yet perfected, the technology is in place and is being developed.

BT is carrying out experiments in the medical world, including surgeons supervising operations by videophone and clinicians holding outpatients' clinics by videophone to enable people in more remote geographic locations to attend with a clear reduction in the clinician's or the patient's travelling time.

To have a videophone requires use of the Integrated Services Digital Network (ISDN). Unlike a regular telephone line which has one 'channel', an ISDN line has two. In the case of the videophone both channels are needed. Both parties need to have the ISDN lines and a videophone comprising a screen to transmit the picture (which can be through a computer or a television screen) and a camera like a mini-camcorder fixed to the top of the screen casing. Then conversations can take place as down the phone line but with the additional visual clues. There are even devices being developed to enable the picture to be seen in 3-D, and BT trials using videophone technology are also exploring this.

Once the equipment becomes more refined, cheaper and easier to access, there is no reason why it could not be explored for counselling too.

Imagine then, working with a client by videophone. It has all the advantages of telephone counselling – such as no geographical barriers, no travelling expenses if the equipment is at home – and I would think there are few obstacles to the counselling process. Indeed, those counselling or psychotherapy orientations which might not be deemed suitable for telephone work because they also rely on the visual body language and the observing of the client during silences could surely be adapted for the video-phone.

It might be feasible for clients to select potential counsellors from a 'videomenu' where counsellors could introduce them-selves, their counselling styles, qualifications, fees and experience. The client could then contact as many counsellors as she or he wished for a further conversation or for a trial session . . . and so on.

Technology is moving fast and anyone who does not choose to keep up with it will surely be left behind. As I write, computer-assisted therapy programmes have been developed and, although currently not widely used in the UK, these are certain to gain wider acceptance.

Being willing to broaden one's horizons and working practices, perhaps in some of the ways outlined in this book, and exploring new methods with an open mind is essential for the development of all counsellors in the late 1990s. It is also essential if we are to be able to offer our clients options for them to consider of the most appropriate medium, ways of working, and the most suitable counsellor or therapist.

Appendix of Addresses

These are the contact addresses for organisations mentioned in the text. They are listed in alphabetical order.

British Association for Counselling, 1 Regent Place, Rugby CV21 2PJ; Tel: 01788 550899; E-mail: bac@bac.co.uk

Broadcasting Support Services, Villiers House, The Broadway, London W5 2PA; Tel: 0180 280 8000

BT Consumer and Environmental Programmes, Procter House, 100–110 High Holborn, London WC1V 6LD; Freephone information line about calling helplines: 0800 0800 08

Cancerlink, 11–21 Northdown Street, London N1 9BN; Tel: 0171 833 2818; Freephone Cancer Information Helpline 0800 132 905; Freephone Asian Cancer Information Helpline 0800 590415. Cancerlink also has an office in Scotland – call London for details

The CareAssist Group Limited, CareAssist Court, Wheatfield Way, Hinckley Fields, Hinckley, Leicestershire LE10 1YG; Tel: 01455 251155

ChildLine, 50 Studd Street, London N1 0QP; Tel: 0171 239 1000

Community Network, First Floor, 50 Studd Street, London N1 0QP; Tel: 0171 359 4594

CRUSE – Bereavement Care, 126 Sheen Road, Richmond, Surrey TW9 1UR; Tel: 0181 940 4818; CRUSE Bereavement Line Tel: 0181 332 7227

Family Policy Studies Centre, 231 Baker Street, London NW1 6XE; Tel: 0171 486 8211

ICSTIS – The Independent Committee for the Supervision of Standards of Telephone Information Services, 3rd Floor, Alton House, 177 High Holborn, London WC1V 7AA; Tel: 0171 240 5511; Fax: 0171 379 4611; E-mail: sarah.harrison@icstis.org.uk

Joseph Rowntree Foundation, The Homestead, 40 Water End, York YO3 6LP; Tel: 01904 629241; Fax: 01904 620072

Justfax, 37 Marshall Street, London W1V 1LL; Freephone: 0800 716909

Kids Telephone Help, Counselling Young People by Phone, Box 513, Suite 100, 2 Bloor Street West, Toronto, Ontario M4W 3EZ, Canada

The Multiple Births Foundation, Queen Charlotte's and Chelsea Hospital,

Goldhawk Road, London W6 0XG; Tel: 0181 740 3519; Fax: 0181 740 3041; E-mail: mbf@rpms.ac.uk

The National Council for Vocational Qualifications (NCVQ), 222 Euston Road, London NW1 2BZ; Tel: 0171 387 9898; Fax: 0171 387 0978

NSPCC Child Protection Helpline, NSPCC National Centre, 42 Curtain Road, London EC2A 3NH; Tel: 0171 825 2500

The Office of the Data Protection Registrar, Wycliffe House, Water Lane, Wilmslow, Cheshire SK9 5AF; Tel: 01625 545700

OFTEL, 50 Ludgate Hill, London EC4M 7JJ

Research Society for Process Oriented Psychology UK (RS POP UK), 34 Narcissus Road, London NW6 1TH; Tel: 0171 433 3704

The Samaritans Headquarters, 10 The Grove, Slough SL1 1QF; Tel: 01753 532713; E-mail: jo@samaritans.org or to maintain anonymity use samaritans@a-non.penet.fi

Scottish Vocational Education Council (SCOTVEC), Hanover House, 24 Douglas Street, Glasgow; Tel: 0141 248 7900

Spinal Injuries Association, 76 St James's Lane, London N10 3DF; Tel: 0181 444 2121; Fax: 0181 444 3761; Counselling Line: 0181 883 4296

The Telephone Helplines Association, 61 Gray's Inn Road, London WC1X 8LT; Tel: 0171 242 0555; Fax: 0171 242 0699; E-mail: 101342.3246@Compuserve.com; Web Site: http://www.point2.co.uk/clients/tha/index.htm

References

Advice, Guidance, Counselling and Psychotherapy Lead Body (1995) *First Release of Standards*. AGCP Lead Body, National Council for Vocational Qualifications, April.

Baxter, Carol (1989) *Cancer Support and Ethnic Minority and Migrant Worker Communities*. London: CancerLink.

Bond, T. (1993) *Standards and Ethics for Counselling in Action*. London: Sage.

Bozarth, J. and Temaner Brodley, B. (1986) 'The core values and theory of the Person-Centred Approach'. Paper prepared for the First Annual Meeting of the Association for the Development of the Person-Centred Approach, Chicago.

Brockopp, G.W. (1973) 'Crisis intervention: theory, process and practice', in D. Lester and G.W. Brockopp (eds), *Crisis Intervention and Counselling by Telephone*. Springfield, IL: C.C. Thomas.

Clarke, D.C. and Fawcett, J. (1992) 'Review of empirical risk factors for evaluation of the suicidal patient', in B. Bongar (ed.), *Suicide: Guidelines for Assessment, Management and Treatment*. New York: Oxford University Press, pp. 16–48.

Condy, Ann (1995) *Family Policy Studies Centre Project to Evaluate Multiple Births Foundation Project: Telephone Consultations within an Advisory Service*. London: Family Policy Studies Centre.

Culley, Sue (1990) *Integrative Counselling Skills in Action*. London: Sage.

Dryden, W. (1992) *The Dryden Interviews*. London: Whurr.

Dryden, W. and Feltham, C. (1992) *Brief Counselling – a Practical Guide for Beginning Practitioners*. Buckingham: Open University Press.

Dryden, W. and Feltham, C. (1995) *Counselling and Psychotherapy: A Consumer's Guide*. London: Sheldon Press.

Egan, G. (1990) *The Skilled Helper: Models, Skills and Methods for Effective Helping*, 4th edition. Pacific Grove, CA: Brooks/Cole.

Fish, Sandra L. (1986) 'The Crisis Hotline as mediated therapeutic communication'. Paper presented to the 72nd annual meeting of the Speech Communication Association, Chicago, Illinois, November.

Fish, Sandra L. (1987) 'Therapy on the telephone: the decentralization of traditional therapy'. Paper delivered at the 95th Annual Convention of the American Psychological Association, August.

Fish, Sandra L. and Gumpet, G. (1990) *Talking to Strangers: Mediated Therapeutic Communication*. Norwood, NJ: Ablex.

Fletcher, Emma (1994) 'Using telephone groups to train volunteer counsellors in a self-help setting'. Dissertation for MSc in Counselling (Supervision and Training), University of Bristol.

Gingerich, Wallace J., Gurney, Raymond J. and Wirtz, Thomas S. (1988) 'How helpful are helplines? A survey of callers', *Social Casework: The Journal of Contemporary Social Work*, December: 634–9.

Horton, Anne L. (1995) 'Sex related hotline calls', in A.R. Roberts (ed.), *Crisis Intervention and Time Limited Cognitive Treatment*. Thousand Oaks, CA: Sage. Chapter 12.

Jacoby, Mario (1984) *The Analytic Encounter – Transference and the Human Relationship*. Toronto: Inner City Books.

Jaffrin, Stéfan (1992) *Les Services d'aide psychologique par téléphone*. Paris: Presses Universitaires de France.

Kagan, N. (1976) *Interpersonal Process Recall: a Method of Influencing Human Interaction*. East Lansing: University of Michigan Press.

Kids Help Phone (1994) *Counselling Young People by Phone: A Kids Help Phone Handbook for Professional and Volunteer Counsellors*. Toronto: Kids Help Phone.

McCarthy, Patricia R. and Reese, Robin G. (1990) 'Crisis intervener perceptions of the stressfulness of caller problems'. Paper delivered at the Annual Convention of the American Psychological Association, August.

McCormick, Elizabeth Wilde (1996) *Change for the Better – Self Help through Practical Psychotherapy*. London: Cassell.

McLennan, J. (1990a) 'Helping counselling trainees to integrate microskills', *Australian Counselling Psychologist*, 6(2): 39–44.

McLennan, J. (1990b) 'Clients' perceptions of counsellors: a brief measure for use in counsellor research, evaluation and training', *Australian Psychologist*, 25: 133–44.

McLennan, J., Culkin, K. and Courtney, P. (1994) 'Telephone counsellors' conceptualising abilities and counselling skills', *British Journal of Guidance and Counselling*, 22(2): 183–96.

McLeod, J. (1993) *An Introduction to Counselling*. Buckingham: Open University Press.

McLeod, John (1994a) 'The research agenda for counselling', *Counselling*, 5(1): 41–3.

McLeod, John (1994b) *Doing Counselling Research*. London: Sage.

Mahrer, A. (1989) *Experiential Psychotherapy: Basic Practices*. Ottawa: Ottawa University Press.

Mearns, D. and Thorne, B. (1989) *Person-Centred Counselling in Action*. London: Sage.

OFTEL (Office of Telecommunications) (1994) *Households without a Telephone*. London: OFTEL.

OPCS (Office of Population Censuses and Surveys) (1992) *General Household Survey* (GHS), annual survey of about 10,000 households in Great Britain. London: OPCS.

Rao, Jammi Nagaraj (1994) 'Follow up by telephone – it may be just as good to talk on the telephone as in a clinic', *British Medical Journal*, 309 (10 December): 1527–8.

Read, B. and Bryan, E. (1995) 'Twins clinic or telephone service? The relative costs'. Paper presented at the Seventh International Congress for Twins Studies, Virginia, USA.

Read, B., Bryan, E. and Higgins, R. (1996) *A Time to Talk: A Telephone Service for Families*. London: Multiple Births Foundation.

Rice, Laura N. and Kerr, Gillian P. (1986) 'Client and therapist vocal quality', in L.S. Greenberg and W.M. Pinsof (eds), *The Psychotherapeutic Process: A Research Handbook*. Guildford Press: New York/London. pp. 77–105.

Roberts, Albert R. (ed.) (1995) *Crisis Intervention and Time Limited Cognitive Treatment*. Thousand Oaks, CA: Sage.

Rogers, Carl R. (1987) *Client-centred Therapy*. London: Constable.

Rosenfield, M. and Urben, L. (1994) *Running a Telephone Cancer Support Group – Evaluation of a Short-term Project*. London: CancerLink.

Ryle, A. (1990) *Cognitive-Analytic Therapy: Active Participation in Change*. Chichester: Wiley.

Salminen, S. and Glad, T. (1992) 'The role of gender in helping behaviour', *Journal of Social Psychology*, 132(1): 131–3.

Sanders, Pete (1993) *An Incomplete Guide to Using Counselling Skills on the Telephone*. Manchester: PCCS Books.

Sanders, Pete and Liptrot, Damian (1993) *An Incomplete Guide to Basic Research Methods and Data Collection for Counsellors*. Manchester: PCCS Books.

Talmon, M. (1990) *Single Session Therapy*. San Francisco: Jossey-Bass.

The Telephone Helplines Association (1993) *Guidelines for Good Practice in Telephone Work*. London: Telephone Helplines Group/Association.

The Telephone Helplines Association (1995a) *Helpline Evaluation – Guidelines for Helplines Seeking to Conduct an Evaluation of their Service*. London: Telephone Helplines Group/Association.

The Telephone Helplines Association (1995b) *Calling Helplines*. London: Telephone Helplines Group/Association (leaflet).

The Telephone Helplines Association (1996) *Telephone Helplines Directory First Edition*. London: Resource Information Service.

Wallbank, Susan (1994) *Counselling by Letter – Guidelines for Good Practice*. CRUSE Bereavement Care.

Waters, Judith and Finn, Eric (1995) 'Handling client crises effectively on the phone', in A.R. Roberts (ed.), *Crisis Intervention and Time Limited Cognitive Treatment*. Thousand Oaks, CA: Sage. Chapter 11.

Index

Compiled by Meg Davies (Registered Indexer)